I0625779

Understanding Your Sleep Struggles

Shared Lessons from an Insomniac

Brandon Meisner

Staten House

Copyright © 2025 by Brandon Meisner

Staten House Publishing with M&W Publishing

All rights reserved.

No portion of this book may be reproduced in any form without written permission from the publisher or author, except as permitted by U.S. copyright law.

For D. S. Wright.

Thank you for supporting my sleepless nights.

Contents

This publication reflects the personal insights, opinions, and perspectives of its author. Its purpose is to offer valuable and enlightening content regarding the subjects of sleep and insomnia. Readers should recognize that the author does not provide medical, health, or any form of professional advice within these pages. It is advisable for readers to seek guidance from qualified medical or health professionals before implementing any suggestions or drawing conclusions based on the material presented. The author explicitly disclaims any liability for any potential losses, damages, or risks—personal or otherwise—arising from the use or application of the information contained herein.

Introduction

I nsomnia is a prevalent condition that affects countless individuals, myself included. It involves difficulties in both falling asleep and maintaining sleep, often resulting in waking up prematurely. The impact extends beyond mere sleep deprivation; it also leads to persistent fatigue during the day. The effects of insomnia extend beyond just not sleeping well. Day after day, the fog of fatigue clings to me. Simple tasks can feel overwhelming when I haven't rested properly. My focus fades, and I become irritable. During a busy workday, this fatigue can make it hard to pay attention or engage with colleagues.

Over the years, I have sought to comprehend the underlying causes of this issue and explore potential solutions. For more than two decades, I have endured sleepless nights. Every night, I face the challenge of restlessness. Lying in bed for hours, staring at the ceiling, is exhausting. Sometimes, I feel like my mind is racing with thoughts that won't quiet down. Other times, worrying about the next day keeps me awake. This struggle has taught me a lot about myself, and about sleep. This book encapsulates everything I have discovered during those sleepless hours (days, actually). Please note that I am not a medical professional or licensed healthcare provider, I am simply an individual who has faced years of sleeplessness, and want to share what I have discovered.

Everyone is different. Some of the strategies that I use, may not work for you, but I hope I have listed enough ideas that you will find something helpful in the following pages. There will be some repetition in discussing these strategies, because often topics do overlap when discussing sleep remedies. I hope this tactic you will not find annoying, but helpful. Try to remember that sleeping just *one* night is not the goal, it is to alter the habits that keep you awake ongoing...it is the journey that is important. (Although I do know how one good-night's-sleep can make all the difference!) Throughout my journey of over 20 years trying to find the elusive "Sandman", I have discovered many practical strategies that can lead to better sleep. I have collected all these ideas, strategies, theories, and have assembled them into one place -and I will share them in the pages to follow....Because I understand the challenges you face.

A Shared Journey

Through my journey with insomnia, I have learned invaluable lessons about sleep and well-being. By understanding the challenges and implementing practical strategies, I have taken steps toward better sleep. The path may not be easy, but with patience and knowledge, it is possible to find a way forward. I invite you to explore this topic further, and continue seeking restful nights.

As I write this book, I hope to connect with others who face similar challenges. You are not alone! Insomnia can feel isolating, but knowing that others understand what you are going through can provide comfort. I understand the hours laying awake in bed at night, staring at the ceiling as your mind races. I understand walking around your house in the middle of the night like a ghost when everyone else is sleeping. I understand how it feels the next day at work having to pretend to be alert, when you are exhausted. By sharing my experiences and the things I have learned, I hope to provide support and encouragement to those on a similar path. Again, it's important to remember that we are not alone in this battle against sleeplessness.

Personally, the fight against insomnia is ongoing. While I have made progress, there are still nights when sleep eludes me. Acknowledging this reality helps me be kinder to myself during tough times. On those difficult nights, I try to fall back on the strategies I have developed and researched.

Through this research, I have gained invaluable insights into the realm of sleep, and my intention is to share this knowledge, systematically compiled in this comprehensive book. Ironically, I spent many sleepless nights thinking about writing this book, and am glad to finally get it all out of my head and share with you everything I have compiled.

I sincerely hope this book proves to be helpful for you. If it happens to be too dull and lulls you to sleep, then I couldn't be happier!

Chapter 1

Understanding the Need for Sleep

I tossed and turned, staring at the clock as the minutes ticked away. It was one of those nights where sleep felt elusive, as if actively avoiding my call for rest. I had tried everything—flip-flopping to find the right position, adjusting the temperature, even counting sheep—but nothing could coax myself into that blissful state of slumber. The irony wasn't lost on me; I knew the reasons why sleep was essential. Yet here I was, wide awake, a testament to how complex and finicky getting a good night's sleep could be.

If you are reading this book, I know you understand. For many adults like me and you, understanding the roots and importance of sleep can be both enlightening and frustrating. We often brush off sleep problems as minor nuisances despite knowing their impact on our daily lives. This chapter delves into the fascinating exploration of why we need sleep from both historical and biological perspectives. Discovering these underlying reasons offers valuable insights into why maintaining healthy sleep patterns is crucial, not just for productivity but for overall well-being.

Understanding the Biological Necessity of Sleep

When you lie down, head sinking into the pillow, your body is just getting started on a night's worth of critical tasks. The restoration happening behind closed eyelids is profound. Sleep acts as a full-on maintenance team for both your physical health and mental well-being. Without it, you'd quickly find yourself muddling through life in a fog of forgetfulness and sluggishness. Each sleep cycle plays a pivotal role in helping you recover from the day's wear and tear. When your body hits the pause button and moves into sleep mode, it repairs cells and tissues, boosting muscle growth and protein synthesis, which are essential for repairing physical damage.

The necessity of sleep for mental restoration is equally important. Cognitive functions, the mental processes by which we gain knowledge and understanding, depend heavily on getting enough sleep. Such functions include memory and decision-making—two critical things we need every day. When you get a good night's sleep, you're more likely to remember what you learned and, importantly, how to apply it. Studies show that the brain uses sleep to consolidate memories, embedding new information into long-term storage. It's like an updating and defragmenting process for your hard drive up there. Without sufficient sleep, this process is interrupted, resulting in concentration lapses and forgetfulness the next day.

Sleep deprivation doesn't just leave you feeling foggy-headed; it can lead to significant cognitive impairments. With too little rest, the brain struggles to operate properly. Neurons get over-taxed and can't coordinate information properly, leading to memory lapses, decisions made in haste or error, and decreased reaction times. Worse still, chronic sleep deprivation is linked to increased risks of mental health issues like depression and anxiety. The emotional volatility from not having enough rest compounds into stress that can spiral out of control. You might find yourself struggling with even the simplest problem-solving tasks or getting irrationally upset by minor setbacks.

Physiologically, the body needs sleep to manage and regulate numerous essential processes. During sleep, your immune system is busy producing protective immunological agents like cytokines. These are vital for combating infections and inflammation. If you're run down and sleep-deprived, your immunity weakens, leaving you vulnerable to illnesses. Even recovery from existing illnesses takes a hit, potentially prolonging any episode of ill health. Plus, sleep influences metabolic functions that regulate appetite. Disruption in sleep patterns often leads to an imbalance in the hunger hormones, ghrelin and leptin, contributing to weight gain and an increased risk of obesity.

Crucial repair processes also occur while dreaming away. Hormones, like growth hormone, are released at their highest levels during deep sleep, crucial for growth and cell regeneration. Human growth hormone is paramount for muscle repair, bone strength, and metabolism regulation. Sleep serves as a reset button that circulates this fountain of youth in the body each night. Simultaneously, taking a nighttime break gives your heart and blood vessels a much-needed rest, reducing the stress they endure throughout the day. Not enough sleep can lead to heart diseases, high blood pressure, diabetes, and stroke.

Viewing this within an evolutionary context, sleep's role in conserving energy begins to reveal itself. While modern life may make it less noticeable, our ancestors had to carefully manage energy resources for survival. Therefore, the act of sleeping—reducing our responsiveness and awareness—was evolutionarily beneficial because it decreased the energy demand during periods of inactivity or danger. Resting isn't just about recovery but imbued with the purpose of surviving longer with energy-efficient strategies.

The metabolic rate reduction during sleep is a finely tuned activity orchestrated by the body to conserve energy. Your body uses fewer calories when you're asleep. Breathing, heart rate, and body temperature drop, resulting in an overall decline in metabolic activities that could otherwise deplete energy reserves. The body prioritizes energy savings while maintaining only critical processes, akin to running a laptop on power-saving mode during low battery.

With this groundwork understanding of sleep's biological necessity, you are well poised to explore the upcoming discussion on how sleep plays a pivotal role in energy conservation. It offers a bridge into understanding why our bodies need to retreat into this vulnerable state night after night. Sleep supports the intricate balance of life by managing health and resource conservation, crucial aspects no different today than they were for our ancestors. Sleep is not merely a luxury or a passive state but an indispensable activity honed by evolution to foster longer, healthier lives.

The Role of Energy Conservation in Sleep

In our ongoing exploration of sleep's role in energy conservation, we find ourselves delving deeper into its essential function in human survival. Sleep, as an evolutionary adaptation, has ensured that humans and animals alike manage their resources efficiently. The act of sleeping lowers our metabolic rate, essentially putting the body into a low-power mode, which aligns perfectly with the notion of conserving energy for times when it is most needed.

During sleep, the body reduces energy expenditure significantly. The heart rate slows down, breathing becomes regular, and body temperature drops slightly. These physiological changes reduce the overall demand for calories, illustrating one of nature's clever strategies for energy management. Scientists have likened this to turning down a thermostat, saving fuel for when it is more urgently required. For instance, the restorative power of sleep allows our bodies to repair cells and tissues, clear toxins from the brain, and conserve a substantial amount of energy which would otherwise be expended in staying awake and active.

Understanding these unique biological mechanisms reveals how sleep has evolved as a necessary function to balance the demands of energy usage. From an evolutionary standpoint, this concept likely played a pivotal role in survival, allowing our ancestors to conserve energy during the night, a time when foraging or hunting was less efficient or even hazardous. During these quiet hours, instead of engaging in energy-intensive activities, sleep provided a way to reduce metabolic demands, preserve caloric reserves, and remain safe from nighttime predators. Over millennia, sleep thus became hardwired into our biological rhythms, shaping behavioral patterns and daily routines.

The evolutionary benefits of this energy conservation strategy extend beyond basic survival. In modern contexts, this translates to why individuals with healthy sleep patterns often lead more energetic and productive lives. Sleep ensures that upon waking, individuals have both the cognitive and physical energy required to tackle the day's challenges. This underscores the importance of sleep hygiene and presents a persuasive argument for integrating sufficient rest into health-conscious lifestyles.

Moreover, the comparison of sleep to other biological processes, such as hibernation or torpor in animals, further underscores its significance. While humans don't hibernate, the parallels are evident. Bears, for example, lower their metabolic rates during hibernation to preserve energy throughout the winter when food is scarce. Similarly, bats enter torpor to conserve energy during inactive periods. These examples from nature illustrate an overarching strategy across species: survival through strategic energy conservation. Sleep in humans and these energy-conserving processes in animals share a common thread of efficiency, showcasing nature's ingenuity in sustaining life.

Understanding how energy conservation during sleep translates into modern human advantages redefines our approach to rest. A well-rested individual is equipped with more energy, sharper focus, and better decision-making skills. Sleep provides the body and mind the opportunity to recalibrate, effectively preparing individuals to navigate an increasingly complex world. This physical and mental replenishment is particularly vital in environments demanding constant attention and critical thinking.

This leads us naturally into an exploration of how sleep fosters memory consolidation and learning. During sleep, the brain engages in a symphony of activities to reinforce learning and store memories. The transition from energy conservation to cognitive enhancement is crucial. It's during the deepest stages of sleep, particularly during REM (Rapid Eye Movement - not the band), that the brain processes information from the day, solidifying new skills and knowledge. This process, integral to memory consolidation, underscores the cognitive advantages of sleep.

Studies have shown that sleep after learning a new task enhances the ability to perform that task more effectively. The body of research connecting sleep with improved memory retention and problem-solving serves as a compelling motivator for making sleep a priority. Establishing a habit of getting adequate sleep leads to better school performance, increased work productivity, and enhanced creativity.

Memory consolidation involves the transformation of information from short-term to long-term memory. While individuals sleep, memories get replayed and reinforced, forming a stable and enduring record that assists in future retrieval and application. This fascinating work of the mind suggests a cerebral organization and filtration system that prunes unnecessary details while prioritizing valuable insights. Thus, understanding sleep's role in this context reveals its profound impact on our ability to learn and adapt.

It is critical to acknowledge how these cognitive benefits empower us in every facet of our everyday lives. From improved focus and creativity to better problem-solving skills, sleep is the unsung hero behind many of our intellectual capabilities. This understanding of sleep elevates its position from being merely a necessary rest period to an active component in our cognitive success.

Prioritizing sleep becomes not just a question of personal health, but a strategic decision that fosters lifelong learning and progression. By recognizing and valuing these aspects of sleep, we are encouraged to adopt more disciplined sleep practices, ensuring that we maximize both our energy conservation and cognitive potentials.

In conclusion, by recognizing the interplay between energy conservation and cognitive enhancement, we better appreciate sleep's comprehensive role in enhancing human life. The transition from conserving physical resources to nurturing intellectual growth seamlessly integrates the understanding that sleep is a cornerstone of a balanced and fulfilling life. Transitioning to our next focus, let's delve into the vital role sleep plays in enhancing memory and cognitive function, further illuminating the necessity of integrating robust sleep habits into our daily routines.

Sleep and Cognitive Health

Recent discourse on sleep's role in energy conservation naturally guides us to consider the cognitive realms of memory and learning. While conserving energy undeniably aids survival, cognitive returns from sleep enhance the quality of life. We see sleep acting as more than a biological recharge; it's a significant contributor to our intellectual and emotional health.

Research demonstrates that sleep reinforces memory consolidation and bolsters learning capabilities. Think about it. How often have we heard someone say they'll sleep on it to make a decision? Science backs this up. Studies show, after a good night's sleep, our ability to retain information boosts significantly. Take, for example, a relevant study conducted by researchers at the University of Lübeck in Germany. Participants who slept after learning new tasks showed a marked improvement in performance compared to those who remained awake. Sleep, they found, enhances the brain's ability to formulate connections and insights that go undetected during waking hours.

You may have noticed you remember an event's details better after a good night's sleep. This happens because sleep allows our brain to process information as we slumber, transferring important facts from short-term to long-term memory. Research from Harvard Medical School emphasizes sleep's role in this memory consolidation process. It turns out, sleeping after learning something new fortifies that knowledge. People recall details and understand concepts better after sleeping well. This cognitive benefit is powerful motivation for adults to adopt healthier sleep habits.

We've touched on studies showing the physical benefits of sleep, such as energy conservation. But the cognitive benefits deserve equal attention. For example, one study highlighted in *Nature Neuroscience* linked sleep deprivation to impaired cognitive performance. The findings suggest even one sleepless night can hinder our problem-solving skills and creativity. When we think about the negatives of inadequate sleep, we see how fundamentally it affects our brain's efficiency in learning or retaining information.

Let's consider learning. Evidence confirms that students who prioritize sleep perform better academically. Take teenagers, for instance. A published study in the *Journal of Clinical Sleep Medicine* reveals students who sleep more than eight hours a night achieve higher grades than their tired counterparts. The benefits of sleep extend beyond test scores. Adequate rest keeps students more attentive, engaged, and productive during classes, in turn fostering a more conducive learning environment.

It's clear that sleep affects cognitive function, but why do we often neglect this critical aspect of sleep health? Modern society tends to downplay the necessity of sleep in favor of work or entertainment. We've all been guilty of it, but understanding cognitive benefits changes everything. Knowing that sleep not only affects health but directly impacts how we perform intellectually and emotionally, we can start to make more informed choices. Health organizations, educators, and corporations are beginning to shift priorities, acknowledging sleep's role in success as seen through programs that educate employees and students on good sleep practices.

While the biological need for energy conservation establishes the baseline for sleep, the cognitive perks are arguably what enhance our existence. Memory consolidation, learning capacity, and retention—these aren't just academic exercises. They affect daily life, relationships, and personal achievements. Imagine preparing a presentation, only to find yourself drawing a blank because of poor sleep. Had those hours been borrowed from another activity, you could've delivered more confidently and convincingly.

Sleep isn't a mere downtime. It's an active period when the brain works energetically. This understanding can reshape how we approach rest. Quality sleep makes us smarter and more effective. It's an investment in oneself yielding rich benefits. Moreover, a population that acknowledges sleep's importance in cognitive functioning is better situated to innovate and grow.

The conversations around sleep keep evolving. From modern science, we learn its vital role in enhancing brain power. Yet, we've only scratched the surface. Next, let's delve into historical beliefs to grasp the evolution of sleep's significance. Ancient cultures often linked sleep to spiritual dimensions. They recognized it as a bridge between realms of consciousness. By understanding these perspectives, we see how interpretations have shaped modern concepts and the essential practices of sleep hygiene. This journey informs us how early beliefs penetrate contemporary living. It guides us to respect sleep not merely as a biological need but a holistic component of human experience.

Ancient societies often considered sleep sacred, where dreams and reality entwine. With this knowledge, we enrich our understanding of how cultural perspectives evolve, reflecting shifts in values and approaches over centuries. This narrative ties a rich tapestry of past insights to our ongoing quest for a balanced life where sleep is not an indulgence but a necessity.

Exploration of Ancient Beliefs and Practices Regarding Sleep

Previously, we examined how sleep plays a vital role in memory and learning. Understanding its cognitive benefits brings our attention to how contemporary views on sleep often find roots in ancient interpretations. Ancient cultures were well aware of sleep's significance, even if they explained it through different lenses. By taking a look back, we can see how past beliefs continue to influence today's attitudes toward sleep.

In ancient times, many civilizations saw sleep as a sacred time when the soul could connect with the spiritual realm. Ancient Egyptians considered sleep an opportunity for communication with divine beings. Priests often entered dream temples to seek guidance from gods. This reverence can still be seen in the way some cultures maintain practices focused on dreams and spiritual well-being.

Various mythologies across the world tell of gods associated with sleep and dreams, underlining a widespread cultural valorization of sleep. For instance, the Greeks had Hypnos, the god of sleep, who resided in a dark cave where the Sun never shone and took care of refreshment through restful slumber. Similarly, the Roman god Somnus had priests who meditated on sleep's transcendence, seeking prophetic visions. These deities not only show sleep's esteemed status but also illustrate a deeper societal reverence—a reverence that paved pathways for modern sleep concepts.

Historically, many civilizations aligned their sleep patterns with the natural ebb and flow of daylight. Evidence from ancient Rome shows people practiced a biphasic sleep pattern, dividing their slumber into two intervals. The first sleep began shortly after sunset, followed by an awakening around midnight before a second sleep until dawn. Such a schedule reflects life's direct interplay with day and night. In China, the Yin and Yang philosophy highlighted harmony and balance, recommending rest during darkness to align with the natural world.

In India, Ayurveda regarded sleep as one of the pillars of life, advocating sleeping specific hours in sync with the sun's cycle. This respect for nature's rhythm is seen in how modern societies strive for consistent sleep schedules, recognizing their role in enhancing sleep quality.

Ancient healing practices also revolved around improving sleep quality. The Greeks used meditative techniques, breathing exercises, and herbal mixtures to foster better sleep. Likewise, traditional Chinese medicine involved acupuncture and herbs like chamomile for relaxation. The Incas used coca leaves, not only for energizing activities but believed in their powers for helping transition to a state of restfulness (- more on cocoa/chocolate in a later chapter). Civilizations recognized how the natural world contributed to sleep, and their holistic approaches can be seen in how we today explore dietary, environmental, and lifestyle adjustments for better sleep.

As we close this section, we find ourselves transitioning to an era that majorly disrupted sleep traditions—the Industrial Revolution. Advancements in technology, like factory systems and artificial lighting, had a profound impact on sleep patterns and overall sleep quality. Previously respected natural rhythms faced challenges as human work commitments expanded beyond daylight hours. This shift marks significant societal changes that warrant further exploration in the next section.

Understanding these developments sets the stage for examining how drastically altering lifestyles influenced modern sleep experiences. By taking cues from both ancient insights and industrial transformations, we can form a holistic view of sleep that helps better navigate today's challenges.

Industrial and Cultural Influences on Modern Sleep Patterns

Since ancient times, sleep has been shrouded in a mix of mystery and necessity. Ancient civilizations often classified sleep as a mystical process, intertwined with dreams, spiritual visits, and a rejuvenation ritual. Myths and traditions further dictated the timing and nature of sleep as influenced by cycles of lightness and darkness. The fall of night was a sacred signal for rest, unbroken by the glow of gadgets or glaring lights.

Fast forward to the late 1800s/early 1900s, the Industrial Revolution triggered seismic shifts in how society approached sleep. With industries churning out products around the clock, artificial lighting became a functional necessity rather than a curiosity. Gas lamps and electric bulbs soon infiltrated factories and homes, shattering the natural dark-light cycle humans had relied upon for centuries. The rhythm of the work-day transformed, with daylight no longer dictating productivity. Night became an extension of day—work shifts extended into the late hours, forever altering human sleep habits.

Consider the rise of factory work during this era. Previously, individuals shaped their workload around daylight, waking at dawn and winding down at dusk. With industrialization, the introduction of night shifts and round-the-clock production meant that sleep started adapting to the needs of productivity rather than biological clocks. Workers frequently found themselves needing to rest while the world outside was alive and buzzing—a stark contrast to the previous calm that nature once dictated. The resulting havoc on circadian rhythms went largely unrecognized at the time but profoundly impacted sleep quality and health.

Sleep hygiene, a concept that's gained traction in recent years, unofficially began to degrade during this period. Artificial light disrupted more than natural sleep cycles; it also interfered with melatonin production, the hormone responsible for signaling bedtime. The illusion of perpetual daylight fostered environments that encouraged late-night activities, a stark deviation from pre-industrial habits. Sleeplessness increasingly took root as people traded restful nights for productivity's demands and socio-cultural expectations.

Revisiting society's evolving work-life balance, industrial schedules not only lengthened working hours but also reshaped evening leisure. Electric lights allowed people to pursue social activities and entertainment once reserved for daylight. Theaters, taverns, and social gatherings extended late into the night, heralding sleep deprivation as a byproduct of urbanization. This cultural shift paved the way for narratives that sometimes glorified sleepless hustle—a trend that's imprinted itself in today's "always-on" culture.

The Industrial Revolution didn't just tweak individual sleep behavior; it influenced broader cultural narratives about productivity and rest. The notion of "burning the midnight oil" found real meaning, where industriousness symbolized success despite the biological cost. Sleep began to appear expendable, even lazy, in a world striving for economic growth.

This perception persists today, affecting how we value rest in a fast-paced, technology-driven society.

However, the modern world has begun to recognize the toll of this revolution-induced sleep disorder. The vivid comparison of factory and industrial-era work schedules to present-day work-life balance issues highlights a repeated pattern in the societal evolution of sleep habits. We're more aware now of the consequences of tampering with innate cycles. Concepts like "sleep debt" and the significant adverse health impacts of chronic sleep deprivation enter common discourse, shifting narratives yet again.

Examining these historical insights into the transition from ancient practices, through industrial upheavals, to modern developments can enlighten efforts to reclaim sleep health. Increasing awareness of humans' biological wiring and the importance of aligning daily schedules with our internal clocks emphasizes the growing movement toward balance. Sleep hygiene today calls for innovative strategies that echo the natural cycles eco-systems once proudly governed.

To avert another industrial-like disruption, current efforts to nurture better sleep quality focus significantly on minimizing artificial light exposure, particularly the blue light emitted by screens. Re-establishing darkened environments close to bedtime helps re-engage melatonin production, repair the sleep cycle, and enhance overall sleep quality. Additionally, strategic urban planning incorporating more natural spaces and lighting designs that mimic natural environments may assist societal efforts to harmonize modernity with human health.

As we use historical lessons as a lens, we can understand sleep not just as a passive necessity but as an active cornerstone of health. Correcting perceptions regarding sleep isn't an indulgence but rather a critical investment. We can appreciate broader societal trends—we see that while technology revolutionized the night, it has also created opportunities for learning how to prioritize rest.

Communities striving for restful well-being now advocate for flexible work schedules, reduced night shifts, and environments that align with natural rhythms to enhance sleep quality consistently. With these practices, we begin to mend fragmented sleep patterns that centuries of societal evolution misaligned. What once was a mere response to industrial opportunity now calls for intentional adaptation to restore and preserve harmony between lifestyle and sleep.

In the end, understanding these links is essential in shaping solutions for healthier sleep amidst relentless demands. Historic shifts remind us of humanity's capacity to adapt—yet also reflect the genuine need to embrace change carefully. Each generation wields the tools to redefine relationships with sleep, ensuring tales aren't just of agitational past but restful futures crafted with both insight and intention.

Concluding Thoughts

Wrapping up this chapter, it's clear that sleep is more than just a nightly routine; it's a vital part of living well. We've explored how our ancestors saw sleep as sacred and connected to the earth's cycles, showing us the potential benefits of aligning our sleep with natural rhythms. The Industrial Revolution may have steered us away from these practices, but today we're starting to reawaken to the importance of quality rest for both our physical and mental health. With newfound understanding, we can now take steps to reclaim our sleep health by reducing screen time before bed, creating calming evening routines, and respecting our body's need for rest. By integrating these insights into our daily lives, we have the power to enhance our energy levels, cognitive abilities, and overall well-being, paving the way for healthier and happier futures.

Chapter 2

Unveiling the Historical Remedies

In the dim glow of a medieval chamber, a weary soul lay awake, searching desperately for the embrace of sleep. The night stretched endlessly, filled with the quiet hum of crickets and whispers of ancient remedies. On a rough-hewn table nearby, an assortment of herbs—fennel, yarrow, valerian—lay scattered, their earthy scents mingling in the air, promising solace yet failing to deliver it. This scene is not merely of the past; it echoes through time, reflecting a universal struggle that transcends eras and cultures. From the wisdom of Hildegard of Bingen to the age-old practices of the Greeks and Romans, people have long sought to conquer insomnia, using everything from herbal teas to spiritual rituals.

Today, as we unravel these historical attempts to soothe the restless mind, we are reminded that the quest for peaceful slumber is as old as humanity itself. These age-old insights provide a window into how understanding sleep has evolved alongside shifting cultural norms and stressors. In exploring the intricate ties between ancient practices and modern perspectives, we gain valuable insights into how history continues to shape our approach to wellness and rest. By delving into this rich tapestry, we aim to illuminate the enduring challenge of sleeplessness and how the past might hold keys to unlocking better sleep in our contemporary lives.

Historical Remedies for Insomnia

In ancient medical texts, sleep was interpreted through cultural beliefs and medical knowledge. Hildegard of Bingen, a herbalist from the medieval period, provided insights into sleep remedies. Her texts advised using specific herbs for different times of the year: fennel and yarrow in summer, while winter prescriptions varied slightly to meet the season's needs. This attention to detail shows how historical views on sleep were closely linked to cultural and environmental understanding. Hildegard also suggested combining certain herbs with practices like binding them to the head and sprinkling green sage with wine on the heart, reflecting a mix of physical and substance-based remedies. These manuscripts offer health tips and reveal a worldview where body and spirit health were inseparable, highlighting sleep struggles as a persistent human challenge recognized across different cultures.

Herbal treatments have been essential in understanding sleep. Valerian and chamomile were common remedies, known for their soothing effects long before scientific tests confirmed their benefits. Valerian, often used as a tranquilizer, was popular in 19th century America, much like it is today among those seeking natural sleep aids. Chamomile's calming properties made it a staple in textiles and teas. These practices indicate an early acknowledgment of nature's calming effects, aligning with present trends towards natural remedies and wellness solutions. Modern consumers often return to these traditional herbs, linking past practices with current interest in holistic health and improving sleep quality through plant-based approaches.

Various cultures incorporated sleep into their religious and spiritual rituals. The ancient Greeks viewed sleep as influenced by divine forces, with sleep and dream deities central to their belief system. This perspective illustrates how societies have historically regarded sleep not just as a physical necessity but also as essential for spiritual insights and balanced living. The spiritual connection to sleep remains relevant today, as practices like meditation, yoga, and mindfulness utilize rest to enhance overall well-being. These practices recognize the relationship between mental peace and restorative sleep, suggesting continuity in the belief that spirituality and health are interconnected.

Historical methods like baths and massages played a key role in promoting relaxation and improving sleep. Roman baths and Turkish hammams, for instance, combined water therapy and massage to help individuals relax. These methods emphasized the importance of physical relaxation as a precursor to sleep. Today, they continue in spa rituals and home routines, reflecting the longstanding legacy of these practices. Incorporating massages or baths into nightly routines replicates proven methods that support mental tranquillity and restful sleep.

Looking ahead to a discussion on historical views of stress and their influence on modern understandings of sleep and well-being, it is important to recognize how emphasis on ease, tranquility, and holistic practices aligns with growing awareness of stress's impact on health. Historically, sleep remedies aimed not just at inducing sleep but at addressing broader life issues. This legacy continues today, sparking deeper exploration into how historical insights can inform current challenges. Acknowledging stress not just as a factor in poor sleep but as a significant impact on overall health illuminates the ongoing dialogue between past knowledge and contemporary health strategies.

As this section concludes, it transitions to the next topic—how ancient and historical perspectives on stress inform current approaches to sleep and well-being. The following section will examine this evolution, highlighting how awareness of stress's role has developed into a key aspect of today's wellness discussions. This conversation connects historical insights on sleep remedies with modern implications, preparing for further exploration of how our ancestors' challenges and solutions continue to shape our understanding of health and well-being.

Dealing with Stress and our "Animal Nature"

In earlier times, people approached the relationship between stress, daily living, and sleep differently. Moving beyond traditional solutions like herbal remedies, there is a clear link between stress, historically recognized as a major disruptor of sleep, and modern approaches to sleep issues and wellness. Historical observations reveal how the understanding of stress has affected sleep across various cultures. Initially, recognizing stress involved observing human experiences of transition, trauma, and challenges.

Stress as a sleep disruptor can be traced back to ancient civilizations that emphasized spiritual and physical balance. These early viewpoints have striking similarities to today's holistic interventions. Ancient Indian writings highlight Ayurvedic practices that integrated mental balance for better sleep. Similarly, traditional Chinese medicine viewed stress as a disturbance of Qi, or life force, which also disrupted sleep. These beliefs resonate with modern wellness strategies suggesting that harmony among body, mind, and environment can regulate sleep effectively.

From these early perspectives, stress was seen as a physical sign of imbalance that impacted both sleep and overall health. Hans Selye's introduction of "stress" into health psychology in the early 1920s reinforced this idea. By linking stress with physical and emotional disturbances, he provided a basis for understanding its impact on sleep. Selye's emphasis on stress as structural changes rather than solely an emotional experience helped frame it as a tangible factor influencing well-being. His insights enhance today's understanding of physiological stress responses, which disrupt natural sleep cycles.

The acknowledgment of stressors as central to sleep disruption influenced Western theories during the 19th and 20th centuries. Urbanization and industrialization led to a faster-paced lifestyle, increasing stress levels and correlating directly with disturbed sleep patterns. Awareness grew of how daily stresses—financial worries, work pressures, and social tensions—triggered hormonal responses that kept people alert, hindering their ability to rest. It became apparent that modern stressors included complex psychological components in addition to basic threats.

Important developments during this period included psychological theories by Lazarus and Folkman, which positioned coping as a mediator between stress and sleep disturbances. Coping mechanisms became essential for managing stress-induced sleep issues. This perspective drives current cognitive-behavioral therapies that focus on reducing stress to enhance sleep quality.

Cultural interpretations reveal that many indigenous societies viewed sleep in relation to natural rhythms and stressors. For example, Native American tribes understood stress as a disruption to their harmony with nature, linking restful sleep to life balance. In African traditions, communal living and shared responsibilities lessened personal stress, resulting in better sleep. These practices highlighted a collective resilience that shapes community wellness programs today.

Throughout history, different cultures recognized intrinsic stress responses that influenced sleep cycles. This included the natural inclination for midday rests seen in Mediterranean societies and the two-phase sleep pattern of ancient Europe. These historical lifestyles prioritized rest intervals, aligning with natural stress relief mechanisms, contrasting sharply with today's prolonged work hours.

Today, the complex understanding of stress and its effect on sleep forms part of a larger narrative concerning environmental stressors and internal responses that worsen health issues. Modern sleep disturbances are often addressed through wellness strategies that promote alignment with circadian rhythms. Practices such as mindfulness, yoga, and meditation, alongside creating sleep-friendly environments, are informed by historical insights into stress management that aim to revitalize natural sleep through mental relaxation.

Recognizing the historical context of stress in relation to sleep can guide healthier sleep patterns that align with human biology, promoting better health outcomes by addressing stress before bedtime. Reflecting on the evolution of stress awareness emphasizes its role in creating sleep wellness strategies and the importance of incorporating ancient wisdom into contemporary practices.

The upcoming analysis will examine how historical lifestyles influenced sleep patterns, distinguishing between nocturnal and diurnal behaviors. This will provide an understanding of the broader impacts lifestyle choices have on sleep, illustrating that daily activities significantly affect rest.

Nocturnal vs. Diurnal Lives

Reflecting on the ways stress and societal norms around work have evolved, it becomes evident how much our understanding of sleep has been influenced by the pressure of continuous productivity we've adopted over generations. Historically, the industrial revolution marked a shift in work patterns with its demand for efficiency around the clock, laying the groundwork for common misconceptions such as the necessity of eight hours of sleep. The purported ideal has cultural and historical roots that deserve a closer look, particularly given the rigid expectations we've internalized.

Industrialization catalyzed a significant transformation in daily routines, primarily centered around optimizing labor force efficiency. As people moved from agrarian lifestyles, which were more aligned with natural day-night cycles, to factory work defined by relentless schedules, societal norms around sleep altered dramatically. Nights stretched longer with the widespread introduction of electric lighting, allowing work and social activities to extend well beyond sunset. This shift required adapting our biological clocks to social clocks, a misalignment contributing to what researchers now identify as social jetlag (Smit et al., 2019). The circumstances forced us to assess our sleep less as a variable necessity and more in a structured eight-hour expectation, echoing a sense of uniformity bespoke to effective industrial output.

Yet, this eight-hour sleep idea emerged not merely from necessity but was also buttressed by early scientific investigations. Theories around ideal sleep duration began rooting in the observations of the well-heeled society who, free from the looming demands of industrial labor, could afford leisure and adherence to personal whims about rest. This characteristic separation between work-induced sleep schedules and leisure-inspired notions facilitated the myth of continuity into modern-day sleep culture. The eight-hour metric gained traction, considered almost sacrosanct, almost as if sleep was a commodity measured in hours of standard production, much like the mechanized processes of factories. It illustrates the artificial compartmentalization of rest into socially dictated portions rather than catering to natural, individual rhythms.

This belief, however, does not hold universally. Historical records from traditional societies, unhinged by the pressures of industrial schedules, offer a counternarrative. For instance, indigenous and rural communities in places like Tanzania, Namibia, Bolivia, and Papua New Guinea demonstrate varied sleep durations, reflecting adaptive lifestyles rather than rigid schedules (Smit et al., 2019). Their experiences challenge the eight-hour benchmark by showcasing that sleep need varies and is often less than the universally espoused duration. These discrepancies invite scrutiny of the belief that there is a one-size-fits-all sleep segment necessary for well-being.

Furthermore, rigorously examining these historical trends raises questions about cultural myths that drive collective perceptions around sleep.

With modern economic pressures encouraging longer working hours, associations have surfaced between insufficient sleep and numerous lifestyle diseases (Lee et al., 2021). Sleep duration intertwines with other health behaviors, muddling our understanding of causality. The illusion of standardized sleep has led many individuals astray, striving to fit their varied sleep needs into a monolithic structure shaped not by health but by changing environmental demands and interpreted scientific observations.

So intertwined are these cultural and historical paradigms, they incite individuals to evaluate their sleep environment or routines critically. Exploring how deeply entrenched this sleep ideal has become allows for a deeper inquiry into the adaptability of human rest patterns. Allegiance to societal norms encourages standard expectations, fostering a profound impact on how one measures personal health against collective standards. In contrast, recognizing that duration is merely one aspect of quality rest directs a spotlight on more personal determinants, such as lifestyle, stress, and how they disturb sleep phases.

Acknowledging these pervasive myths compels us to reevaluate our night time routines. It becomes apparent that the belief in an eight-hour mystique of sleep may not align with real-world variances. Understanding prescriptive sleep habits as sensitive to social and historical context liberates us from a reactive belief system. It encourages a nuanced appreciation for tailoring sleep to personal needs, more in line with bodily signals rather than perpetuated societal commandments. For instance, those transitioning to environments with extended evening light exposure noted a shift in sleep patterns; light remains a potent mediator of both timing and perceived restfulness (Smit et al., 2019).

So, as we delve deeper into unraveling the fabric of what constitutes ideal rest, it is important to explore how cultural narratives around the eight-hour notion pervade individual perceptions. Bridging this discussion with upcoming explorations into sleep myths, we anticipate expanding the discourse to include individual tales, those everyday narratives challenging sleep expectations ingrained in cultural constellations. By revisiting the individualization of these practices, the window opens on reconsidering sleep paradigms, shaping them to fit with biological and emotional balance instead of a manufactured sense of adequacy. Thus, as we advance, our journey through the chapter promises to unveil how questioning these set sleep timelines ignites personal revelations instrumental in redefining modern sleep practices in society's vast and evolving landscape.

Origin of the 8-Hour Sleep Myth

Our discussion has previously touched upon historical lifestyles and their effects on sleep. This section explores the historical roots of our contemporary sleep beliefs, particularly the idea of needing 8 hours of continuous sleep. Historically, people have varied widely in their sleeping patterns, influenced by their nocturnal and diurnal activities. These traditional patterns often ran counter to the modern inclination towards 8 uninterrupted hours of sleep. In earlier times, our ancestors may have engaged in a biphasic pattern, consisting of two shorter periods of sleep with a period of wakefulness in between. This approach demonstrates an adaptive response to environmental factors, such as temperature and light (CNN, 2022). By examining these practices, we can gain insight into how contemporary expectations about sleep might have formed and evolved over time.

As industrialization gained momentum, work lives dictated more consistent and demanding schedules. This societal shift necessitated changes not only in work but also in leisure, creating a more structured approach to daily life. Sleeping in a single, long block became idealized as part of this restructuring, leading to the broader cultural expectation of 8-hour sleep durations (Cheung et al., 2021). These changes reflect an adaptation to new social norms, economic demands, and technological advancements that continue to feed into the ongoing narrative of sleep behaviors. In contrast to this, the inventor Thomas Edison believed "sleep was a waste of time", and limited his sleep to often four hours per night, balanced with mid-day naps.

Early scientific scrutiny played an instrumental role in shaping this 8-hour mantra. It was grounded in a view of sleep efficiency and health benefits and further enmeshed in cultural narratives. Studies of sleep initially sought to find optimal periods for physical and mental rejuvenation. Scientists determined that an 8-hour sleep cycle most effectively supported these processes. Despite genetic and lifestyle differences among individuals, this idea became ingrained as a scientific average rather than a personalized goal. Sleep was thus measured quantitatively rather than understood qualitatively in many cultures (Cheung et al., 2021).

These developments also led to widespread storytelling that reinforced the idea. Folklore, myths, and literary works began to romanticize the pursuit of a solid 8 hours, often linking it to productivity, morality, and success. Cultural tales portrayed how successful individuals adhered rigorously to these sleep routines. This storytelling manifested societal pressures where sleep became not just a health necessity but a competitive, even moral, measure.

For instance, Japanese cultural attitudes towards sleep diverge starkly from Western norms. Many in Japan view sleep as a luxury rather than a necessity, often associating a lack of sleep with increased discipline and moral strength. Expressions like *"pass with four, fail with five"* illustrate a belief that sacrificing sleep is vital for academic and professional success (Cheung et al., 2021). This contrasts with the Western embrace of 8-hour sleep under the label of health and well-being, showing how culturally constructed these sleep norms can be.

Inemuri, a unique Japanese concept, refers to the practice of being awake while simultaneously appearing to be asleep or taking a brief rest, often in public settings. This cultural phenomenon highlights the balance between hard work and the need for rest in Japanese society. Inemuri is not seen as a sign of laziness; rather, it symbolizes dedication and the acknowledgment of one's physical and mental limits. People engaging in inemuri, such as dozing off during meetings or on public transportation, embrace the idea that rest is essential for productivity and well-being. This notion reflects the broader values of harmony and balance in Japanese life, where taking a moment to recharge amidst the demands of work is not only accepted but also respected.

As research advances, it challenges previous narratives, advocating for an understanding of sleep that's tailored individually. This new discourse encourages a departure from societal norms, recognizing the wide variety of sleep needs across different people and cultures. The Japanese example demonstrates that, while the 8-hour sleep norm is deeply established in some cultures, others deviate significantly without apparent detriment to their overall health or efficiency (Cheung et al., 2021).

Understanding Sleep Needs

Sleep is often thought of in terms of a standard eight-hour block, but this approach may not suit everyone. Inflexible sleep guidelines can lead to problems, especially for those who have unique needs. To address these needs, it's essential to look for signs in one's daily life that can indicate how much sleep is actually necessary. These signs can include daytime sleepiness, energy levels, and your overall sense of well-being.

Key Signs of Sleep Needs

One important sign to pay attention to is daytime sleepiness. If you find yourself nodding off during the day or struggling to stay awake during tasks, it might be a sign that you aren't getting enough rest. For example, if you feel tired even after a night of sleep, it could indicate that you need more than the recommended amount. On the contrary, if you wake up feeling refreshed and alert, it could mean that the amount of sleep you are getting meets your personal needs.

Energy levels also play a crucial role in determining sleep requirements. A simple way to assess your energy levels is to notice how you feel throughout the day. If you often feel energetic and focused during your activities, that might suggest you are sleeping adequately. Meanwhile, if your energy levels dip significantly around mid-afternoon, it might be telling you that your sleep schedule needs adjustment, possibly increasing the duration of rest.

Another essential factor to consider is your overall health. People who are under stress or dealing with physical health issues might find that their bodies require different amounts of rest to recover and function well. For instance, someone recovering from an illness or undergoing a stressful period might benefit from more sleep compared to their regular routine.

Personal Sleep Preferences

Personal experiences with sleep can provide insight into what works best for you. For instance, I have learned that my body feels best with around ten hours of sleep each night. However, this is specific to my individual needs and preferences. Each person is different; finding your ideal sleep duration requires attention and experimentation. It's important to listen to your body and understand its cues over time.

Discovering Your Optimal Sleep Duration

To find out what amount of sleep works best for you, start by tracking your sleep patterns. You can keep a sleep diary for a couple of weeks. Record the time you go to bed, when you wake up, and how you feel each day. Note any patterns, such as feeling more rested after certain sleep durations. This method allows you to gather concrete evidence about how different amounts of sleep impact your daily life.

Consider also adjusting your sleep gradually. If you suspect you need more sleep, try going to bed 15 to 30 minutes earlier than usual. Give your body time to adjust and observe how you feel after a week. You can continue this process until you find the right balance.

Moving Beyond Myths

Recognizing that sleep needs vary greatly among individuals can help dismantle common myths about sleep. Many people may feel pressured to conform to the idea that eight hours is the only way to ensure good health. However, acknowledging that some may need more or even less can foster a healthier attitude towards sleep. This understanding empowers individuals to pursue strategies that are tailored specifically to them.

Additionally, it's worth noting that the quality of sleep matters as much as the duration. It's possible to sleep for eight hours and still wake up feeling tired if the sleep is of poor quality. To improve sleep quality, consider establishing a calming bedtime routine. This may include winding down with activities like reading, meditation, or gentle stretches. You might also limit screen time prior to bed, as blue light from devices can disrupt the natural sleep cycle.

Customizing Your Sleep Strategy

Tailoring your sleep strategy can aid in achieving better health outcomes. Try creating an environment conducive to sleep. This could involve making your bedroom dark, quiet, and comfortable. If you live in a noisy area, using earplugs or a white noise machine can be helpful. Also, consider adjusting the room temperature to a setting that feels comfortable for you, as this can influence how deeply you sleep.

Nutrition also plays a role in sleep quality. Eating lighter meals closer to bedtime can help prevent discomfort that might interfere with sleep. It's advisable to avoid heavy or spicy foods in the evening. Additionally, be cautious with caffeine and alcohol intake, as these substances can disrupt your sleep patterns.

The Importance of Sleep Consistency

Another essential aspect of sleep health is consistency. Try to go to bed and wake up at the same time every day, even on weekends. This consistency helps regulate your body's internal clock, making it easier to fall asleep and wake up feeling refreshed. Over time, you may find that your body responds better to this routine.

Understanding and addressing individual sleep needs is vital for optimal health. As you take steps to tailor your sleep habits, be mindful of how your body responds. This ongoing process will allow you to refine your approach and take charge of your sleep health effectively. By listening to your own patterns and preferences, you can cultivate a sleep routine that best supports your life and activities.

Moreover, it is arguably more beneficial to emphasize sleep quality over quantity. For example, creating a conducive sleep environment—reducing blue light exposure from screens before bed, maintaining a consistent sleep schedule, and ensuring a comfortable sleep setting—could prove more impactful than merely aiming to extend sleep duration (CNN, 2022).

Recognizing sleep's fundamental role in physiological and mental recovery underscores the potential harm of rigid sleep myths. Sleep deprivation, in any variation, can lead to cognitive decline, mood disorders, and even long-term health issues. Thus, it's vital to approach sleep like a mosaic where each individual puzzle piece enhances the whole. This understanding offers a path to wellness that integrates but does not solely rely on cultural expectations of sleep.

Furthermore, in this ever-evolving landscape of sleep study, it is crucial to remain open to new findings. Sleep science is progressively revealing complexities within the sleep process, providing critical nuances to our understanding of what constitutes "enough" sleep. Regular engagement with these evolving insights allows people to make informed and adaptive choices without being bound by outdated or culturally constrained narratives (Cheung et al., 2021).

Ultimately, engaging with sleep as a deeply personal and dynamic aspect of life empowers individuals to align practices with true personal well-being, discarding the rigidity of inherited myths. By doing so, we elevate our capacity for customization in health practices, leading to a more nuanced appreciation of cultural and personal differences in sleep philosophies. Above all, it's crucial to remember that adapting sleep to fit individual needs—not societal dictates—is crucial for genuine health and satisfaction.

In summary, as sleep continues to be an area of expansive study, it prompts reconsideration of longstanding beliefs and mythologies. Rather than adhering strictly to an 8-hour regimen, focusing on quality, personalized sleep, and integrating ongoing discoveries into daily practices enhances overall well-being and fosters a healthier engagement with sleep itself.

Final Insights

The exploration of historical perspectives on sleep, stress, and societal norms reveals a rich tapestry of practices that have shaped modern understanding and approaches. Throughout history, the integration of nature-derived remedies, spiritual connections, and physical relaxation techniques highlights humanity's enduring quest for restful sleep amidst life's challenges. These age-old insights underscore a fundamental awareness of the interplay between cultural beliefs and health, resonating with contemporary inclinations towards natural and holistic wellness solutions. By recognizing these historical contexts, we can appreciate the diverse influences that contribute to our sleep practices today. As we look forward, embracing this legacy (and finding your own sleep practices) offers the opportunity to refine our approaches to sleep and well-being, integrating both ancient wisdom and modern innovation in our pursuit of better health outcomes.

Chapter 3

Mental Barriers to Sleep

Emma lay in bed, her eyes wide open as the clock ticked past midnight. Her mind was a whirlwind of thoughts, each more pressing than the last. She replayed an awkward conversation she had earlier in the day with her boss, mentally crafting the perfect comeback that eluded her at the moment. As exhaustion crept in, thoughts about an upcoming presentation bubbled to the surface, casting shadows over any hope for rest. The more she tried to command her brain to silence, the louder it seemed to become, amplifying every worry and insecurity until sleep felt like an unattainable luxury.

Many find themselves in Emma's shoes, where mental barriers stand between them and a peaceful night's sleep. These invisible weights can transform bedtime into a battleground of stress and anxiety. Questions loom: Why do our minds refuse to quiet down when we need rest most? Can these cycles of overthinking be broken? In this chapter, we'll delve into the profound connection between mental states and sleep, exploring how to alleviate the burdens that hinder restful slumber and foster healthier sleep patterns.

Understanding Mental Weights and Their Impact on Sleep

Unresolved mental weights can significantly disrupt sleep, leading to restless nights. At bedtime, thoughts about unresolved issues often surface, preventing the mind from finding the peace needed for restful sleep. Our mental states, especially when burdened by negativity, can transform normal pre-sleep routines into stages set for anxiety, which in turn can evolve into a state of hyperarousal (Lin et al., 2025; Robinson et al., 2023). Addressing these mental burdens is essential for achieving healthier sleep patterns.

One common mental weight is the cycle of negative thought patterns that trigger anxiety. When you lie in bed, replaying conversations or worrying about future events, your mind can become a breeding ground for anxiety (Lin et al., 2025). This anxiety not only makes sleep elusive but can also lead to a self-perpetuating cycle where worry leads to sleep deprivation, which fuels further worry the next day. For example, consider someone who fixates on potential job insecurities before sleeping.

Such fixation can escalate anxiety, preventing restful sleep and setting up a cycle of continued unrest and worry.

Cognitive Restructuring

A practical approach to dismantling these negative thought patterns is cognitive restructuring. This method involves identifying and challenging these thoughts and replacing them with more constructive reflections. Here's how it works:

1. **Method**: Cognitive restructuring aims to change distorted thinking and improve emotional regulation.

2. **Detailed Steps**: Start by identifying a negative thought that commonly surfaces before sleep. Next, challenge this thought by examining its validity. Ask yourself questions like, "What evidence supports this thought?" and "What evidence contradicts it?" Then, replace the negative thought with a more balanced one. For instance, if you think, "I'll never finish tomorrow's work," shift it to, "I'll plan my tasks and seek help if needed."

This process of cognitive restructuring can significantly enhance sleep quality by alleviating mental burdens that contribute to anxiety and hyperarousal (Bai, 2023).

Self-compassion plays a crucial role in managing mental loads. Often, we are harsh on ourselves, leading to an internal dialogue that intensifies mental burdens. By practicing self-compassion, we foster a more understanding and kinder approach to our shortcomings, reducing the mental strain that can interfere with sleep. Adopting self-compassion involves acknowledging that everyone struggles and that self-critique is not an effective strategy for improvement. For instance, if you underperform at a task, instead of berating yourself, practice self-kindness by affirming that learning from mistakes is a part of growth.

Journaling

Analyzing sleep patterns and maintaining a journaling practice can significantly impact sleep quality. Tracking nightly experiences and observing daily actions help recognize patterns leading to sleep problems. This awareness directs us toward actions that manage sleep more effectively. Sleep disturbances often stem from lifestyle habits that go unnoticed. By tracking sleep and related activities, we identify triggers such as late-day caffeine, irregular sleep schedules, or stress from work carried over into nighttime routines (Scullin et al., 2018). The information obtained gives us a clearer picture of what disrupts our sleep.

Journal your thoughts to bridge a gap between daily stress and restful sleep. Use it as a tool for emotional release and mindfulness. Writing worries before bed can free your mind, diminish anxiety, and promote relaxation, helping you mentally unwind. The concept of writing thoughts down might seem counterintuitive at first. How could focusing on worries lead to peace? Yet, studies show that this practice improves sleep latency and quality (Pennebaker & Smyth, 2016). For many adults, facing emotional stressors compromises sleep quality, making emotional health vital in pursuing restful nights. By engaging in this reflective practice, you create a form of passive resistance against insomnia and disturbances. Furthermore, crafting an ideal bedtime scenario through journaling combines emotional preparedness with tangible action, bridging the gap faced by those struggling with rest.

Structuring this habit requires a clear routine. Set aside time before bed as part of winding down. In practice, this means dedicating 10-15 minutes each evening to jot down thoughts, worries, or plans for the next day. Address these as part of a comprehensive approach to relaxation. When you write, focus on transferring these worries onto paper, diminishing their mental burden. Frame your journaling around positive nightly intentions. Focus on today's achievements, no matter how minor. Ending your journaling sessions this way works as a mental reset, creating a hopeful mindset conducive to sleep. Imagine a peaceful night, visualizing a calm sleep environment and your ideal rest. Such visualization fosters a mental landscape that aligns with restful sleep.

Journaling provides the powerful technique to offload mental burdens. By writing down your thoughts and worries, you can psychologically distance yourself from them, thereby reducing their impact on your sleep (Lin et al., 2025). Here's how you can incorporate journaling into your routine:

1. **Method**: Use journaling as a tool for stress reduction and mental clarity.

2. **Detailed Steps**: Set aside 15 minutes each evening for journaling. Begin by writing freely about any concerns or feelings you have. No need to edit or critique—let the words flow. After this, shift to a stress-reducing prompt, like writing about a positive event from the day or a goal achieved. This helps in reinforcing a positive mental framework before bedtime.

Gratitude

The Importance of Gratitude Practices

Gratitude practices play a significant role in our mental well-being. They act as a counterbalance to the mental weights that we often carry. These weights can come from stress, anxiety, or negative thoughts. When we engage in gratitude, we are taking a moment to reflect on the good things in our lives. This can be as simple as appreciating a sunny day, a friend's support, or even a delicious meal. The act of recognizing these positive aspects can create a shift in our mood.

Recognizing the Positive in Everyday Life

Focusing on gratitude requires intentionality. It's not just about saying thank you; it's about truly recognizing what you appreciate. One effective way to practice this is by keeping a gratitude journal. Each day, you can write down three things that you are thankful for. They can be big or small, but the key is to be specific. For example, instead of writing "I'm thankful for my family," you might write, "I'm thankful for my sister's call today that made me laugh." This practice not only helps reinforce positive feelings but also encourages you to look for goodness regularly.

Another method is to practice mindfulness. This means being present and fully engaged in the moment. When you eat a meal, take a moment to savor each bite. How does it taste? How does it feel? Appreciating these small experiences can enhance your overall sense of joy. When you focus on these moments, it naturally shifts your thoughts away from what's troubling you.

The Mood Boost from Gratitude

Recognizing and appreciating the positive aspects of your life does wonders for your mood. Psychological studies indicate that individuals who regularly practice gratitude tend to have higher levels of happiness. They report feeling more positive and content with their lives. The impact is also visible on a physiological level. Gratitude can lead to reduced stress levels, helping us better manage the challenges we face daily.

Taking time to acknowledge what you are grateful for can even set the stage for better sleep. When you go to bed with a sense of appreciation, it can quiet negative thoughts that might otherwise keep you awake. Instead of replaying the day's worries in your mind, you redirect your focus to moments of joy and gratitude. To facilitate this, consider ending your day with a brief reflection. As you lie in bed, think of three things that went well that day or things that you deeply appreciate. This simple ritual can foster a more relaxed state of mind, making it easier to drift off to sleep.

Practical Steps to Incorporate Gratitude

There are several actionable steps you can take to incorporate gratitude into your daily life. First, start a gratitude jar. Take a moment each day to write down one thing you are thankful for on a small piece of paper. Place it in the jar. Over time, you'll have a visual representation of the good in your life. When days are hard, you can revisit the jar and read through the notes to remind yourself of your blessings.

Next, consider sharing your gratitude with others. Send a text or write a letter to someone who has made a positive impact on your life. Expressing gratitude strengthens relationships and adds to your sense of belonging. It can be as simple as telling a friend how much you value their friendship. When you let others know they are appreciated, it not only boosts their mood but also reinforces your own sense of connection.

Engaging in group gratitude activities can also be beneficial. Gather friends or family and spend a few moments sharing what you are grateful for. This not only cultivates a positive atmosphere but can also inspire others to adopt gratitude practices in their lives.

Understanding the Impact of Gratitude on Well-Being

Understanding how gratitude works can deepen your practice. It helps to know that gratitude influences our perspective. When we focus on positive elements, it creates a mental framework that prioritizes joy. Over time, this can change your overall view of life. Instead of our minds drifting towards the negative, practicing gratitude helps us build a belief system centered around appreciation.

Furthermore, gratitude has been shown to improve resilience. In challenging times, those who practice gratitude are better equipped to handle stress. They are more likely to seek solutions and recover from setbacks. This resilience is not just beneficial for individuals; it can create a ripple effect in families and communities. When gratitude becomes a shared practice, it fosters a culture of support and optimism.

Building a Habit of Gratitude

Turning gratitude into a habit takes time and consistency. One way to build this habit is to link it with existing routines. For example, if you have a morning coffee ritual, use that time to recall what you are grateful for. Associating gratitude with a daily activity helps reinforce the practice until it becomes second nature.

It may also be helpful to set reminders. A gentle nudge on your phone can serve as a cue to redirect your thoughts towards gratitude. This could be a simple message like "What are you grateful for today?" Over time, you will find that the habit solidifies, and expressing gratitude becomes a more instinctive part of your day-to-day life.

In summary, engaging in gratitude practices is not just beneficial; it can significantly transform your outlook and well-being. By intentionally appreciating the positive aspects of life, you shift your focus away from negativity and create a fulfilling life experience. Here's how to cultivate a gratitude practice:

1. **Method**: Use gratitude exercises to shift focus from mental burdens to positive aspects.

2. **Detailed Steps**: Dedicate a moment before sleep to list three things you're grateful for. These can be simple, like a pleasant conversation or a favorite meal. By actively acknowledging these positive experiences, you create a buffer against the day's stresses, promoting a sense of contentment and relaxation conducive to sleep.

As we venture into the next section, prepare to explore how mindfulness techniques can address anxiety and promote restorative sleep. Mindfulness involves maintaining a moment-by-moment awareness of thoughts, feelings, bodily sensations, and surrounding environments. This practice shows promising results in managing mental burdens and enhancing the quality of sleep.

Linking these interventions back to the psychological mechanisms that stress and anxiety trigger, it's clear how intertwining practices like cognitive restructuring, self-compassion, journaling, and gratitude can help us manage our mental burdens (Chen, 2022; Cheung et al., 2017). Each practice not only addresses specific issues but also helps build a more resilient mental state overall, setting the stage for the mindfulness techniques to come.

These strategies emphasize the connection between mental burdens and sleep quality, guiding readers to recognize these factors as crucial disruptions. Effectively managing these mental weights requires a combination of strategies. By practicing cognitive restructuring, self-compassion, journaling, and gratitude, you pave the way for better sleep and, ultimately, a more balanced and healthy life.

Stress and Anxiety: Unraveling Their Effects on Sleep

Stress and anxiety are potent disruptors when it comes to sleep. The cycle begins with a stress trigger causing the brain to release stress hormones like cortisol. These hormones prepare the body for action, known as the fight-or-flight response, but in the process, they significantly hinder the body's ability to relax. Over time, stress affects both mind and body, creating a cycle where stress causes sleeplessness, which in turn leads to more stress (Palagini et al., 2024). Breaking this cycle is crucial for better rest.

Many individuals encounter challenges where persistent thoughts exacerbate stress and anxiety, hindering their ability to fall asleep or remain asleep. Personally, I often find myself restless at night when laying in bed thinking about tomorrow's activities. I become preoccupied with a work presentation, impending business travel, or reminders like, *"Don't forget to do X tomorrow."* My mind cycles through the details of my To-Do List or the specifics of my presentation, intensifying my anxiety and disrupting my bedtime routine, ultimately resulting in insomnia. This scenario highlights how anticipatory anxiety can disrupt sleep patterns. To address this issue, I keep a small notepad beside my bed. When thoughts arise that I want to recall the next day, I jot them down (with a handy light pen I discovered on Amazon), eliminating the need to turn on the lights. This practice allows me to release these thoughts before they overwhelm my ability to relax.

Mindfulness offers a promising avenue for those struggling with stress-induced insomnia. As a tool for managing stress and anxiety, mindfulness works by anchoring the individual in the present moment, which disrupts the cycle of endless worrying about the past or future (Health, 2024). This technique is particularly powerful at night when the day's stressors can translate into wakefulness.

To practice mindfulness, begin by finding a quiet, comfortable place to sit or lie down. Close your eyes and bring your attention to your breathing. Simply observe each inhalation and exhalation without attempting to change it. Most people find it helpful to count each breath up to ten and then start over. Should your mind wander, gently refocus on your breath without self-judgement. Practicing this regularly can lead to profound improvements in sleep quality, as it retrains the mind to focus on the present rather than racing thoughts (Palagini et al., 2024).

Many individuals have found that mindfulness can drastically reduce insomnia. One success story involves a young professional dealing with relentless bed-time stress. After committing to a short mindfulness practice each night, she observed a notable decrease in her anxiety levels, allowing for significantly better sleep. These real-life experiences demonstrate that, with consistency, mindfulness can become an invaluable component of a nightly routine.

Stress management also benefits from cognitive techniques fostering mental flexibility and reducing overthinking. One such technique involves cognitive restructuring, a process of identifying and challenging negative thought patterns. This involves recognizing irrational or exaggerated thoughts and reframing them in a more balanced way. By changing your internal dialogue, you can lessen the anxiety that often disrupts sleep.

Incorporating these changes hinges on establishing self-help routines. For example, set a pre-sleep ritual that involves mindfulness and cognitive exercises. Create an environment conducive to sleep by eliminating distractions like electronics. Aim for a quiet, cool, and dark setting. Consistency is key; adhering to these routines can help signal the brain that it's time to wind down (Health, 2024).

***

Daily habits also play a fundamental role in managing stress-induced insomnia. Regular exercise, healthy nutrition, reducing caffeine and alcohol intake, and creating a sleep-friendly environment all support better sleep. By integrating these habits into your lifestyle, you create a foundation for improved sleep hygiene (Health, 2024).

For those whose stress levels remain high during the day, mindfulness and stress management should extend beyond bedtime. Techniques such as progressive muscle relaxation, deep breathing exercises, and setting aside time for leisure activities can mitigate daytime stress, making the transition to sleep more seamless.

In scenarios where lifestyle adjustments and mindfulness do not deliver the desired improvements, professional help may be necessary. Cognitive

Behavioral Therapy for Insomnia (CBT-I) is a well-documented treatment that combines behavioral tools and cognitive strategies to treat insomnia, including that induced by anxiety. Seeking professional guidance ensures a tailored approach to your unique needs (Health, 2024).

The journey to manage stress-induced insomnia is multi-faceted. From mindfulness to lifestyle changes, the aim is to create a psychological and physical environment supporting rest. As stress management practices become more integral to daily life, sleep patterns can improve, facilitating not only a good night's sleep but also overall better health. As you explore these approaches, remember that earlier habits and perceptions about sleep, like counting sheep, may not be effective. The subsequent discussion will delve into more productive techniques, offering fresh insights into advancing your sleep strategy.

Myths and Techniques: Choosing Effective Sleep Strategies

Years ago, a popular belief suggested that counting sheep could help someone fall asleep. I tried this, because I thought the idea is straightforward: mentally picture sheep leaping over a fence, and after enough repetitions, I might drift off. However, evidence suggests (and I have experienced) this method actually does more harm than good. Instead of offering a relaxing experience, it may enhance mental activity, counterproductive to achieving restful sleep. The human brain thrives on engaging, creative thought. Counting sheep, a rote and monotonous task, can inadvertently trigger rumination. As you focus on these repetitive thoughts, you may unwittingly incite a cycle of overthinking, making it harder to reach a state of relaxation necessary for sleep.

In reality, passive techniques that induce relaxation far surpass active mental tasks like these. Shift attention to methods like visualization exercises, deep breathing, and progressive muscle relaxation. Visualization involves creating calming mental images that divert the mind from stress. Picture a serene beach sunset or blooming meadow, inviting a tranquil mental landscape that distracts from anxious thoughts. Engage the five senses to enhance this scene; feel the sun's warmth, hear gentle ocean waves, smell salty air, see the vibrant colors, and taste the fresh breeze in your imagination. This sensory engagement helps pull you away from racing thoughts, and guides the mind to a serene state.

Deep breathing offers another path to relaxation by calming the nervous system and promoting a sense of ease. The 4-7-8 method, for example, requires inhaling for four seconds, holding the breath for seven, and exhaling for eight. This paced breathing shifts the body into a restful state, guiding the nervous system toward calmness. Focusing on the breath steadies the mind, creates a meditative space, and weakens anxiety's grip.

Progressive muscle relaxation offers a structured method for releasing bodily tension and promoting mental calmness. This technique sequentially targets muscle groups, tensing and then relaxing each set of muscles from head to toe. By the time you finish, a profound sense of physical relaxation helps quiet the mind. For those whose stress manifests physically, this kinesthetic focus can be a game-changer, converting tension into relief and giving the mind space to unwind.

Research supports these alternatives over common myths like counting sheep. Studies show that relaxed mindfulness significantly boosts sleep quality, linking decreased anxiety with techniques like visualization, breathing exercises, and muscle relaxation. Anderson (2018) notes that regular practice of such methods results in large sustained improvements in sleep. Stress and anxiety, often perceived as inevitable barriers, become manageable with appropriately chosen strategies.

Incorporating feedback from those who have successfully used guided imagery before bed can offer valuable insight. They describe how shifting focus to serene mental pictures redirected anxious thoughts, improving sleep onset rates. **Experimentation and personalization** are key; what helps one person may not work for another. Exploring different relaxation exercises helps discover a routine that best enhances an individual's sleep quality.

Consistency plays an essential role in conditioning the mind. Establishing a nightly routine that integrates relaxing practices reconditions responses to bedtime. The mind begins to associate these exercises with approaching sleep, gradually easing into a more restful state over time. Cultivating regular habits reinforces these connections and optimizes nightly relaxation rituals, breaking mental barriers to sleep.

Breaking down specific relaxation exercises and fostering an understanding of mental state management advances individual sleep health. Highlighting alternative practices to counting sheep not only disproves a myth but provides practical support for readers striving for better sleep quality. Emphasizing consistency, exploration, and personalization encourages growth and rest, essential for both physical and mental well-being. Thus, rather than counting sheep, embrace techniques that truly coax the mind to rest.

Cognitive behavioral therapy for insomnia (CBT-I)

CBT-I is a 6- to 8-week treatment plan to help you learn how to fall asleep faster and stay asleep longer. This method is often suggested my medical practitioners as an alternative to medications and herbal remedies (discussed in Chapter 7). This is usually suggested as the first treatment option for long-term insomnia and can be very effective. CBT-I can be done by a doctor, nurse, or therapist; you can do it in person, by telephone, or online. It involves the following parts:

- **Cognitive therapy** helps you feel less nervous about not being able to sleep.

- **Relaxation or meditation therapy** teaches you how to relax and fall asleep faster.

- **Sleep education** helps you learn good sleep habits.

- **Sleep restriction therapy** gives you a specific amount of time to spend in bed, even if you are not able to sleep during this time. With time, this helps you sleep better when you go to bed. Your sleep time can be increased when you start to sleep better.

- **Stimulus control therapy** helps you have a regular sleep-wake cycle so you can link being in bed with being asleep. This involves going to bed only when you are sleepy, getting out of bed if you cannot sleep, and using your bed only for sleep and sexual activity.

Wrapping Up

As we continue our journey through understanding how mental states impact sleep, we can now appreciate the profound ways unresolved mental weights and stress influence our nightly rest. By identifying and addressing these burdens, whether through cognitive restructuring, self-compassion, or mindfulness practices, we lay the groundwork for healthier sleep patterns. These strategies offer not only solutions to immediate sleep disruptions but also foster long-term resilience against anxiety-induced insomnia. Now that we've explored these interventions, readers are empowered to incorporate them into daily routines, transforming restless nights into restful, rejuvenating experiences. Moving forward, integrating these insights into your life will pave the way for improved sleep quality, contributing to a better-balanced, healthier lifestyle overall.

Chapter 4

Understanding Genetic Influences

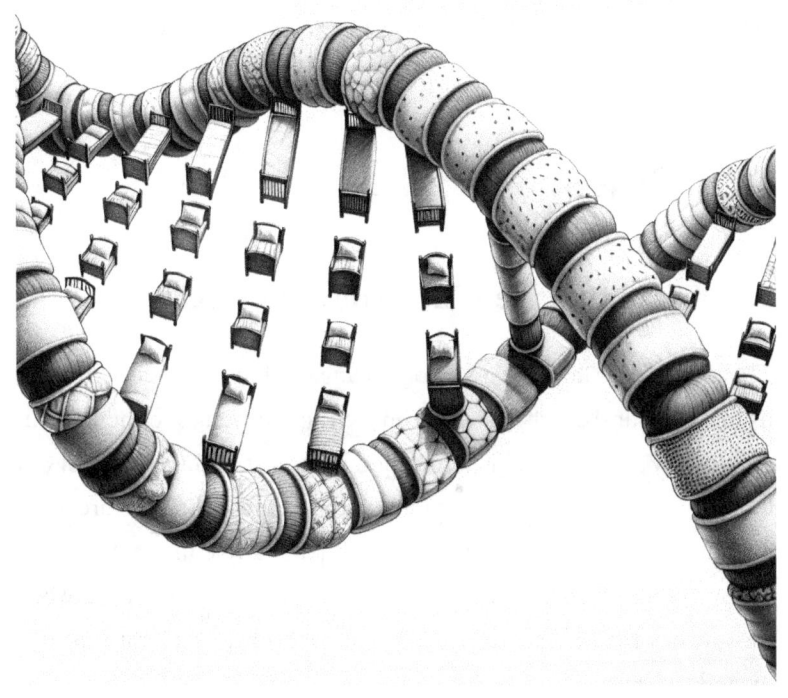

Have you ever found yourself lying awake at night, staring at the ceiling, wondering why sleep eludes you while others seem to slip into slumber effortlessly? I know I have...and it makes me so angry and jealous. Have you questioned why some people can wake up feeling refreshed, ready to tackle the day, while you struggle through mornings with groggy eyes and a weary mind? It makes me feel like I'm missing something important about how my body work, and leave me caught in a restless cycle that seems impossible to break.

In this chapter, we will dive deep into the science of sleep, exploring the physical factors influencing your nightly rest. You will learn about the genetic and biological components that shape your sleep patterns, and perhaps find answers to those relentless questions about your own sleeping struggles.

PER Gene and its Effects

Understanding the PER Gene and Its Role

The PER gene is important for controlling our biological clock. It helps us manage our daily rhythms by connecting our bodies to the 24-hour cycle of day and night. This connection is not just a minor aspect of our lives; it deeply affects our behavior, alertness, and feelings of tiredness. The protein produced by the PER gene plays a role in synchronizing various processes in our body with the time of day. For example, when the sunrises, the PER gene helps signal to our body that it is time to wake up and be active.

Every person has a unique version of the PER gene, which means its effects can vary widely from one individual to another. This variability can lead to different sleep patterns. Some people are early risers, waking up with the dawn feeling energized and ready to start their day. Others may identify more with night-time, thriving during the late hours while finding mornings tough. The way we respond to the time of day is often linked to our genetics, particularly the variations found in the PER gene.

Circadian Rhythms Explained

Circadian rhythms are our body's natural patterns that repeat approximately every 24 hours. These rhythms help dictate when we feel awake and when we feel sleepy. The PER gene is at the heart of this process. It produces a protein that accumulates in our cells throughout the day, reaching its highest levels at night. As the night goes on, this protein eventually breaks down, helping to send signals to our body that it is time to rest.

For many people, understanding circadian rhythms can help improve sleep habits. By recognizing their natural rhythms, individuals can create routines that align with their body's needs. For instance, someone who knows they are a morning person might schedule important tasks for the early hours when they feel most alert. Meanwhile, a night owl could plan activities for later in the day when they are more energized.

Genetic Variations in the PER Gene

Genetic differences in the PER gene can significantly change how individuals experience their days. Research suggests that some variations can affect sleep timing, leading to conditions like delayed sleep phase disorder. This condition can make it challenging for individuals to fall asleep at a typical bedtime, causing them to miss out on rest.

Take the example of two people with different PER gene variations. One person, proactive in managing their schedule, uses their early waking habit to exercise and prepare for the day ahead. Meanwhile, the other struggles to wake up and may feel groggy for several hours. Recognizing these different genetic influences is essential for developing strategies to manage sleep and productivity.

Adjusting Sleep Habits

Given the significant role of the PER gene in our sleep patterns, adjusting our sleep habits can create positive changes. Individuals can start by establishing a regular sleep schedule that aligns with their natural inclinations. This means going to bed and waking up around the same time each day, even on weekends. Consistency can help stabilize circadian rhythms and promote better sleep quality.

Additionally, creating a relaxing bedtime routine can signal to the body that it is time to wind down. Activities such as reading a book or practicing mindfulness can help to calm the mind and prepare for sleep. It is also essential to limit exposure to screens before bedtime. The blue light emitted by phones and computers can interfere with the production of melatonin,the hormone responsible for sleep.

The Importance of Natural Light

Exposure to natural light during the day also plays acritical role in influencing the PER gene's function. Natural light helps our body recognize day from night. Thus, spending time outdoors, especially in the morning, can strengthen our circadian rhythms. This could be as simple as taking a short walk or having breakfast by a window.

On the other hand, it's also beneficial to reduce light exposure in the evening. In a world filled with artificial lights, finding ways to create a dark environment in the evening can prepare the body for sleep.Using blackout curtains or dimming lights can help signal that nighttime is approaching.

Recognizing Personal Patterns

Understanding one's own sleep patterns can make a significant difference in improving sleep quality. Keeping a sleep diary can bean effective way to track sleep habits and identify the best times to sleep and wake. Individuals can note the times they go to bed, how long it takes to fall asleep, and feelings of alertness or tiredness throughout the day.

After a few weeks of tracking, individuals can look for patterns in their data. Noting when they feel most awake or sleepy can provide valuable insights into their personal circadian rhythms. For example, someone might discover they are most productive in the early afternoon rather than feeling that pressure to work in the morning.

Seeking Professional Help When Needed

Sometimes, despite taking steps to improve sleep,individuals may still struggle. If persistent sleep issues arise, seeking professional help can be beneficial. Sleep specialists can provide personalized assessments and treatment plans tailored to individual needs. They may recommend therapies, dietary changes, or lifestyle adjustments that align with a person's unique sleep patterns. (More information about finding a healthcare provider in Chapter 11)

Being proactive about sleep health can lead to better overall well-being. Recognizing the interconnectedness of the PER gene and sleep habits offers an opportunity for individuals to take charge of their sleep. By understanding how genetics influence sleep timing and quality, we can create environments and routines that benefit our unique patterns.

Understanding these genetic nuances can empower individuals to take control of their sleep routines and environments. For instance, if someone discovers they are genetically predisposed to be a night owl, they might focus on creating a bedtime routine that aligns with their natural inclinations rather than forcing themselves into an unwanted early schedule. By embracing their genetic predispositions, individuals can reduce the frustration and guilt often associated with struggling against their natural sleep patterns(Parish, 2013).

Genetic mutations in the PER gene are not just academic curiosities. They have profound implications for sleep disorders. Research highlights the association between these mutations and conditions like insomnia. Insomnia, with its frustrating cycle of fatigue and wakefulness, can often feel uncontrollable. However, recognizing the genetic elements at play offers a different perspective. Rather than attributing poor sleep to personal failings, individuals can look to genetics for explanations and hope for tailored treatments. This understanding could open paths to therapies that consider the unique genetic makeup of each person, encouraging approaches that are both personalized and effective (Pavithra et al., 2024).

Our genes don't sit idle as we age. The expression of the PER gene changes, influencing our sleep as we grow older. Ageing affects more than just the body's exterior; it alters the very architecture of sleep. The shift from deep, uninterrupted sleep to more fragmented patterns is often a common complaint among older adults. These changes can be attributed to age-related shifts in PER gene expression. Life's stages bring new challenges and adapting sleep routines to accommodate these changes is crucial. Evidence suggests that understanding these shifts fosters actionable insights, like adjusting bedtime routines or creating environments that support restful sleep despite a body's changing needs (Parish, 2013).

Lifestyle choices also significantly impact the expression and functioning of the PER gene. Our daily habits—diet, exercise, exposure to light—directly influence our hormones and sleep-related genes. Here's where the power of agency comes into play. Consider how regular physical activity can enhance the PER gene's expression, promoting better sleep quality. Or how reducing screen time before bed can minimize disruptions in our circadian rhythms. Making conscious lifestyle modifications integrates seamlessly with maintaining good sleep hygiene. Healthy habits, such as going to bed at the same time every night, creating a peaceful sleeping environment, or limiting caffeine intake, support our genetic predispositions and improve overall wellness (Pavithra et al., 2024).

Our exploration into the PER gene sets the stage for an upcoming discussion on DMT release patterns and their influence on sleep cycles.

DMT, or dimethyltryptamine, plays a role in dream states and deeper sleep stages. Understanding how DMT interacts with the PER gene's influence offers a more comprehensive view of sleep biology. By appreciating the synergy between genetic influences and sleep-inducing chemicals, individuals can gain a balanced perspective on the complexities of their sleep. As we delve into DMT'sinvolvement, the insights gathered here will act as a foundation, enhancing the comprehension of how these varying elements contribute to or resolve sleep issues. Integrating this understanding offers more holistic approaches to achieving restful, restorative sleep, ultimately improving quality of life.

This intricately woven tapestry of genetics, lifestyle, and biochemical influences paints a vivid picture of the biological complexities of sleep. It calls for a thoughtful approach to understanding and optimizing our sleep through informed choices, reflecting a harmony between our biological makeup and environmental interactions. Recognizing this, the pursuit of restful nights transforms from a frustrating endeavor into an enlightened journey,offering practical pathways toward achieving personal sleep wellness goals.Different elements converge like musical notes to form the symphony of a restful night, encouraging a deeper appreciation of sleep in our lives.

DMT Release Patterns

The Body's Internal Clock

Genetic factors play a crucial role in determining our sleep cycles. One important gene to consider is the PER gene. This gene helps regulate the body's internal clock, known as the circadian rhythm. The circadian rhythm is responsible for making us feel awake during the day and sleepy at night. When the PER gene functions properly, it supports a healthy sleep-wake cycle. However, if there are any mutations or issues with this gene, it can lead to irregular sleep patterns, potentially causing problems such as insomnia or excessive sleepiness. It's essential to understand that genetics can influence not only when we sleep but also the quality of our sleep.

The Role of Neurochemicals in Sleep

While genetics plays a significant role in sleep as we discussed the PER gene in the previous section, neurochemical processes are equally important. One of the most interesting neurochemicals associated with sleep is DMT, which stands for Dimethyltryptamine. DMT is a naturally occurring substance found in the human brain. Research suggests that DMT's influence is particularly profound during certain sleep phases. One of these key phases is known as Rapid Eye Movement (REM) sleep. This stage is especially notable for its association with vivid dreaming.

The Connection Between DMT and REM Sleep

REM sleep is a unique phase of the sleep cycle, typically characterized by rapid movement of the eyes, increased brain activity, and vivid dreams. During this time, the brain processes emotions, consolidatesmemories, and engages in problem-solving. This phase is crucial for overall mental health and cognitive function. DMT is believed to play an influential role during REM sleep by enhancing dreaming and possibly facilitating deeper states of consciousness.

To better understand how DMT works in alignment with REMsleep, it's essential to learn more about its effects. When DMT is released, it can create an experience that feels dreamlike, contributing to the intensity and vividness of dreams. You might not consciously realize it, but these intense dreams may help you process feelings and experiences from your waking life. For anyone interested in enhancing their sleep, focusing on the quality of REM sleep could be beneficial.

Optimizing Sleep Patterns for Enhanced REM

If you want to make the most of your sleep, particularly REMsleep, there are several actionable steps you can take. Firstly, establishing a consistent sleep schedule is vital. This means going to bed and waking up at the same time every day, even on weekends. Consistency helps regulate your circadian rhythm, which can improve both sleep quality and duration.

Secondly, create a relaxing bedtime routine. Activities such as reading, meditating, or listening to calming music can signal to your brain that it's time to wind down. Avoid screens, such as phones or televisions, at least an hour before bed, since the blue light emitted can interfere with melatonin production, a hormone that regulates sleep.

Additionally, pay attention to your sleep environment. Ensure that your bedroom is conducive to rest by keeping it dark, quiet, and cool. Invest in comfortable bedding and consider blackout curtains or white noise machines if necessary. A peaceful sleep environment fosters deeper sleep, increasing the likelihood of reaching REM stages.

The Importance of Nutrition and Lifestyle

Nutrition and lifestyle choices also influence sleep quality. Consuming a balanced diet rich in nutrients supports overall health, which correlates with better sleep. Foods high in tryptophan, such as turkey and bananas, can promote the production of serotonin and melatonin, both of which are essential for healthy sleep.

Hydration is another crucial aspect. While it's important to stay hydrated, be mindful of fluid intake close to bedtime to avoid waking up frequently during the night. Regular exercise can also enhance sleep quality; however, it's best to avoid vigorous workouts right before bedtime, as they might be stimulating.

Stress Management and Sleep Quality

Managing stress is critical for a good night's sleep. High stress can lead to an overactive mind, making it challenging to fall and stay asleep. Techniques such as relaxation exercises, yoga, or mindfulness can help calm the nervous system. By incorporating these practices into your daily life,you can create a more balanced mental state that promotes restful sleep.

Consider keeping a sleep journal, tracking your sleep patterns, moods, and any factors that may have influenced your rest. This record can help you identify areas for improvement, allowing you to make adjustments and find what works best for your unique situation.

Embracing the Science of Sleep

The science of sleep is an evolving field, delving into the complexities of how our biology, environment, and lifestyle choices influence our nightly rest. Understanding the connection between factors like the PERgene and neurochemicals such as DMT sheds light on the intricacies of sleep. By exploring ways to optimize your sleep patterns and ensuring you prioritize aspects that promote REM sleep, you can significantly enhance your sleep experiences.

Learning about the science behind sleep can spark curiosity.By understanding why sleep matters, you may feel a greater motivation to take intentional steps toward better sleep hygiene. Recognizing the benefits of improving your sleep can lead to multiple positive outcomes, impacting your mood, productivity, and overall health.

As you dig deeper into your sleep practices, remain open to experimenting with different approaches. The goal is to find what resonates with you personally, whether it's through adjustments in your daily habits or delving into the scientific aspects of sleep. Embracing these changes can be empowering, leading to a healthier and more balanced life.

As we explore DMT's role in sleep, it's essential to consider the specific phases when its production seems to heighten. REM sleep, the stage when dreaming tends to be the most intense, sees an uptick in DMT. This increase plays a part in forming the dreams that can range from the simple to the surreal, adding an exciting layer to our nightly rest. By tuning into this natural rhythm, individuals may consider adjusting their sleep schedules to prioritize REM sleep, perhaps through practices like dream journaling. This technique not only anchors the dreamy experiences into waking memory but can also improve the overall perception and quality of sleep.

DMT's influence does not operate in isolation. Life stylechoices, including diet, exercise, and meditation, play crucial roles in regulating and optimizing DMT release. A nutrient-rich diet with ample sources of essential vitamins supports neurotransmitter health, affecting sleep efficiency. Engaging regularly in physical exercise also influences sleep cycles, promoting deeper and more restorative phases. Meditation, known for enhancing overall mindfulness, could stimulate natural DMT production and support uninterrupted sleep (Why, 2024). Together, these elements advocate for a holistic approach that nurtures both the body and mind, allowing individuals to navigate their sleep experiences with greater awareness and control.

Understanding the complex interplay between DMT, consciousness, and sleep reveals how this neurochemical's impact stretches beyond mere rest. There is an ethereal boundary where waking life and dreams intertwine, often presenting with used clarity or insights that linger beyond the night's first light. The blurred lines that DMT influences invite us to consider the significance of dreams not just as random nightly occurrences, but integral threads in the tapestry of human consciousness. By appreciating how these dynamics unfold, one can gain a more profound perspective on the potential held within each sleep cycle.

Lifestyle modifications that aim to harness the power of DMT in enhancing sleep are well within reach. Consider the influence of dietary choices, where foods rich in tryptophan—a precursor to serotonin and melatonin—bolster sleep quality through neurochemical pathways. Exercise also has a multifaceted impact; not only does it regulate circadian rhythms, but it supports overall mood stability and stress reduction, indirectly influencing DMT's role in sleep (Why, 2024). Furthermore, meditation offers a bridge between conscious relaxation and subconscious exploration, potentially aligning brainwaves such that DMT production is naturally stimulated.

As researchers delve deeper into the connection between DMT and sleep, they increasingly unearth insights that influence wellness practices. More holistic approaches that consider neurochemistry and lifestyle adjustments may well provide pathways to improved sleep quality without reliance on external aids. In this exploration, the focus extends beyond sleep itself, touching on broader elements of well-being. Encouraging this awareness and inviting individuals to make informed lifestyle choices can support sustainable improvements in sleep and elevate overall health.

The conversation about sleep quality naturally transitions to examining the influence of physical activity on rest patterns. Physical exertion, like neurochemicals, plays a fundamental role in shaping sleep experiences. Exercise affects several biological systems, aligning with DMT's influence on REM sleep to enhance rest quality. Exploring how physical activity contributes to sleep efficacy builds upon understanding DMT's influence, offering a cohesive narrative linking physical and mental health across sleep cycles.

Promoting a broad understanding of the factors that influence sleep, including both tangible lifestyle adjustments and intriguing neurochemical activities, engages readers actively in managing their rest. Each night's sleep can become a purposeful exploration guided by dietary choices,exercise habits, and meditation practices that align with the body's natural rhythms and chemical balances. While decoding the interaction between DMT and sleep cycles enriches the scientific narratives surrounding rest, the emphasis remains on how individuals can harness this knowledge to foster well-being in mindful, actionable ways.

By bridging these connections, individuals are empowered to view each component as an integral part of the greater picture of health. DMT illustrates complex neural dynamics that intersect with daily choices, inviting deeper consideration of our sleep's purpose and quality. As we continue fromDMT's profound influences to physical activity's interplay with sleep, we prepare to understand sleep as a dynamic, responsive aspect of living,intimately linked with our behaviors and awareness. Such a perspective may indeed invite transformative as well as restful nights.

Role of Physical Exertion on Sleep

Building on the previous exploration of DMT release patterns that influence sleep, let's delve into how physical exertion and neurochemical processes collaboratively enhance sleep quality. Regular physical activity plays a key role in improving sleep onset and extending total sleep time(Alnawwar, 2023). When individuals engage in consistent exercise, the benefits manifest in various ways, including improvements in the time it takes to fall asleep and the overall duration of sleep experienced each night. Engaging in physical activities doesn't just affect a single aspect of sleep but impacts multiple dimensions, providing a more comprehensive enhancement of sleep quality.

Aerobic activities stand out in this context, contributing significantly to better sleep. Regular aerobic exercises have been linked to pronounced improvements in sleep onset latency and quality. The benefits of these exercises extend beyond immediate physical improvement to neurochemical engagement, which aids better sleep patterns. For instance, morning or afternoon aerobic activities have proven more beneficial than late-night exercises, preventing disruption of sleep onset. This timing matters as it aligns with the body's circadian rhythms, maximizing the potential benefits of exercise on sleep (Alnawwar, 2023).

Moreover, the correlation between higher physical fitness levels and fewer instances of insomnia further emphasizes the role of exercise in achieving restorative sleep. Individuals with varied exercise routines, particularly those incorporating aerobic activities, often report reduced incidences of insomnia. For instance, people who establish a regular routine of moderate to high-intensity exercise, such as cycling or swimming, generally experience fewer sleep disturbances and enhanced overall sleep quality (Ye etal., 2022).

Concrete examples help solidify our understanding of these benefits. Take, for example, a person who incorporates a morning jog into their daily routine. Over time, this consistent physical exertion not only improves their cardiovascular fitness but also leads to more restful and uninterrupted sleep patterns. The explanations for these improvements aren't one-size-fits-all; factors like personal preferences and exercise intensity should guide individual routines. For some, the rejuvenating power of a brisk walk might suffice; for others, an hour-long session of swimming might be the key to a good night's sleep. Tailoring these physical activities to one's lifestyle and preferences ensures better adherence and consequently, better sleep outcomes.

When considering exercise routines, it's crucial to acknowledge the variety and adaptability required to meet individual sleep and health needs. For the well-being of sleep patterns, a blend of different exercises—such as aerobic activities complemented by strength training—might offer the best results, depending on age and fitness level. This diversity not only ensures comprehensive fitness but also maintains motivation and interest in the exercise regimen. Furthermore, it's important to factor in personal schedules and preferences, allowing flexibility in exercise duration and timing to align with daily routines and maximize sleep benefits.

Avoiding redundancy and repetition here ensures a clear understanding of how these factors come together to improve sleep. Emphasizing the variety of beneficial exercises and the nuances of timing and preferences offers a complete picture of how to leverage physical exertion for better sleep. Direct sentence structures support clarity, making it apparent how each element contributes distinctly to boosting sleep quality.

As we pave the way towards the section exploring age-related changes, it's essential to highlight how physical exertion's impact on sleep evolves with age. Younger individuals may find greater immediate effects due to metabolic and hormonal differences, whereas older adults might experience modifications in how exercise contributes to their sleep regulation .Understanding this intersection between physical exertion and age-related sleep changes prepares us to explore further how these dynamics shift and what steps can support sleep health throughout different life stages.

Age-Related Sleep Changes

Physical exercise has profound effects on sleep quality.Previous sections of this chapter detailed how regular physical activity contributes to more restorative sleep by reducing sleep onset latency and increasing the proportion of slow-wave sleep. The impact of exercise extends beyond immediate improvements, fitting into a comprehensive sleep-enhancing strategy that aligns with other physical and lifestyle factors influencing sleep, such as genetics and age-related changes.

Ageing significantly alters sleep patterns. Older adults generally experience shorter total sleep times, increased nocturnal awakenings,and reduced slow-wave sleep (Li et al., 2017). These changes are driven by physiological shifts in the circadian rhythm and sleep homeostasis, as naturally occurring hormones and neurochemical processes responsible for regulating sleep diminish with age. To counteract these changes, individuals must adapt their sleep habits, emphasizing the importance of maintaining a regular sleep schedule despite the potential disruptions ageing may cause (Casagrande etal., 2022).

Understanding the multiplicity of factors affecting sleep can empower older adults to address their sleep challenges effectively.Creating a conducive sleep environment stands out as a foundational step. This includes optimizing the bedroom setting by controlling ambient noise,regulating room temperature, and minimizing exposure to artificial light before bedtime. Such environmental adjustments align with age-related tendencies towards increased sensitivity to external stimuli during sleep (Li et al., 2017).

Lifestyle choices prove equally paramount in supporting sleep health. Diet, for instance, plays an influential role—consuming a balanced diet rich in sleep-promoting nutrients like magnesium and tryptophancan enhance sleep quality. Regular meal timings assist in stabilizing circadian rhythms, which often become less pronounced with age (Casagrande et al., 2022).Additionally, avoiding caffeine and alcohol close to bedtime reduces the likelihood of interrupted sleep.

While these lifestyle modifications can profoundly impact sleep quality, they must be tailored to individual needs. Each person responds uniquely to dietary changes, exercise regimens, and other lifestyle factors due to their genetic makeup. Genetic predispositions can affect everything from an individual's inherent circadian rhythm type—such as being a night owl versus an early bird—to their sensitivity to caffeine. Understanding these genetic influences allows for personalized approaches to enhancing sleep quality.

Equally important is recognizing and addressing sleep disorders, which can become more prevalent as we age. Conditions like sleep apnea obstruct restful sleep, leading to chronic fatigue and other health complications. Proactively managing these disorders involves both medical interventions and personal lifestyle changes. For instance, using CPAP devices for sleep apnea can significantly reduce interruptions during sleep, improving both duration and quality of rest. Moreover, healthy lifestyle practices—including weight management and physical activity—are front-line strategies in mitigating the symptoms of sleep disorders.

Age-related transitions, such as retirement or moving to assisted living facilities, also impact sleep (Li et al., 2017). These life changes can alter daily routines, increase opportunities for napping, and reduce social interaction, contributing to irregular sleep patterns. Encouraging consistent daily schedules that mirror pre-retirement routines can help stabilize sleep patterns. Engaging in social activities and mental exercises can also maintain circadian rhythms and promote sleep homeostasis.

Altering bedtime behaviors offers a direct avenue for improving sleep quality in older adults. Establishing a calming bedtime routine—whether through reading, meditation, or listening to soothing music—signals the body to prepare for rest. These routines can be supplemented with natural or prescribed sleep aids. Melatonin supplements, for example, may help regulate sleep-wake cycles disrupted by age-related changes. However, medical advice should always precede the use of supplements due to potential interactions with existing medications.

Older adults grappling with sleep challenges might find that a more holistic approach is beneficial. This involves integrating physical fitness, environmental optimizations, dietary adjustments, and proactive disorder management into a cohesive sleep strategy. For instance, a daily routine combining morning exercises, a balanced diet, social engagements, and an early evening wind-down routine holistically addresses various factors affecting sleep (Casagrande et al., 2022).

Monitoring sleep patterns can also provide valuable insights for improving sleep health. Utilizing tools like sleep diaries or wearable sleep trackers helps identify patterns and potential disruptions in sleep, allowing individuals to adjust their routines accordingly. Tracking sleep not only increases awareness of sleep behaviors but also provides data that can be shared with healthcare providers to tailor interventions more effectively.

Adults who actively manage these lifestyle factors often experience not just improved sleep quality, but also enhanced overall well-being. Consistent quality sleep boosts cognitive function, enhances mood,and improves physical health, making it an essential component of healthy ageing. Moreover, addressing sleep disruptions early can mitigate their progression into more severe issues, contributing to better long-term health outcomes.

In this chapter, the inter-connectedness of various physical influences on sleep has been explored—from exercise and nutrition to genetic and environmental factors. For adults experiencing sleep issues, understanding these connections and making informed, personalized adjustments can significantly improve sleep quality. As we navigate the complexities of our body's sleep mechanisms, proactive strategies that embrace lifestyle and environmental modifications offer the best prospects for restful, restorative sleep—a cornerstone of enduring health and quality of life in the later years.

Concluding Thoughts

In understanding the profound connection between genetics and lifestyle on our sleep patterns, we find ourselves empowered to take charge of our nightly rest with informed decisions. As the PER gene intricately links with our circadian rhythms, acknowledging its impact allows us to craft routines that honor our natural inclinations, rather than fight against them.By integrating genetic insights with lifestyle choices—like optimizing diet,exercise, and sleep environments—we lay the foundation for better sleep quality. This chapter's journey through genetic influences sets the stage for exploring neurochemical interactions, like DMT's role in REM sleep, as a further layer of understanding. Armed with this knowledge, individuals can customize their approach to achieving restful nights by harmonizing biological predispositions with intentional habits. Now that we've unveiled these genetic underpinnings, we can appreciate the holistic interplay of factors affecting sleep and take deliberate steps towards enhancing overall well-being and vitality.

Chapter 5

Dietary Influence on Sleep

Kevin had always struggled with sleep. No matter how hard he tried, restful nights seemed elusive, leaving him exhausted. His evenings often began with a familiar ritual: a quick dinner consisting of whatever was convenient—usually something processed or sugary. As he lay awake, his mind sporadically drifted into why sleep seemed so evasive for him. Amidst tossing and turning, Kevin pondered if his dietary choices could somehow play a role in these restless nights.

Many adults can relate to Kevin's plight. Sleeplessness remains a common yet puzzling aspect of many lives, with various potential culprits. In the following chapter, we examine the link between our diets and sleep patterns, delving into how specific foods and eating habits might influence the quality of our rest.

Impact of Diet on Sleep

Understanding the impact of dietary choices on sleep patterns and quality highlights the complex relationship between nutrition and sleep health. Sleep, a fundamental aspect of well-being, relies not only on regular patterns but also on the right mix of nutrients to support restorative processes. The distinction between diets rich in nutrients and those filled with empty calories often underlies variations in sleep quality. A nutrient-dense diet, rich in vitamins and minerals, facilitates balanced hormone production that regulates sleep cycles and promotes sound sleep. In contrast, empty calories from sugary and processed foods can lead to sleep disturbances, primarily because they may induce blood sugar spikes and crashes or fail to provide the nutrients that support bodily functions essential for restful sleep (St-Onge et al., 2016).

The Importance of Nutrient-Rich Foods for Sleep

A balanced diet plays a significant role in promoting good sleep. Nutrient-rich foods, such as leafy greens, nuts, and seeds, are essential because they help the body produce melatonin and serotonin. These two neurotransmitters are critical for managing sleep cycles. Melatonin is often called the "sleep hormone" because it signals our body when it's time to sleep. Serotonin, on the other hand, helps regulate mood and contributes to a feeling of calmness. When we consume foods packed with nutrients, we enhance our body's ability to create these important substances, leading to better sleep.

One recent study that was released was the effect of the Kiwi fruit on sleep. The study examined individuals who consumed kiwi before bedtime. Kiwis may help you sleep because they contain serotonin and melatonin, which are brain chemicals that regulate sleep. Kiwis also contain other nutrients that may improve sleep quality. In the study, the researchers wanted to see if eating kiwi had any effect on sleep duration, sleep onset time, and overall sleep efficiency. (Doherty, et al.) Participants were observed over several weeks, with some eating kiwi regularly while others did not consume it at all. The results were quite promising. one of the main findings of the study was that those who ate kiwi reported longer sleep duration. On average, participants who included kiwi in their evening routine experienced more hours of sleep than those who did not. This is significant because getting enough hours of sleep is essential for maintaining good health and cognitive function.

Leafy Greens: A Sleep Aid

One example of a nutrient-rich food is leafy greens. Foods like spinach, kale, and Swiss chard are full of vitamins and minerals. They contain magnesium, which is known to relax muscles and calm the nervous system. Eating a salad with various leafy greens at dinner can help relax your body. This, in turn, may make it easier to fall asleep at night. Try incorporating these greens into snacks or meals to improve your sleep.

One family of vegetables to call-out specifically is garlic and onions, both members of the Allium family. They have been linked to various health benefits, including potential effects on sleep. These aromatic vegetables contain compounds such as sulfur and antioxidants, which may help reduce inflammation and promote better overall health. Garlic, in particular, has been known to possess relaxing properties that may aid in calming the nervous system. Onions, too, contribute to cardiovascular health, which can affect sleep quality. Additionally, their rich content in vitamins and minerals can support immune function, thereby potentially reducing nighttime disruptions caused by illness. While direct research on their specific impact on sleep is limited, incorporating garlic and onions into a balanced diet may indirectly contribute to improved sleep patterns through their numerous health benefits.

Nuts and Seeds: Small but Mighty

Nuts and seeds are another group of foods that can aid in sleep. Almonds, walnuts, flaxseeds, and pumpkin seeds are all packed with nutrients. They are particularly high in magnesium and zinc, both of which contribute to improved sleep quality. For instance, a handful of almonds before bedtime can provide your body with the necessary nutrients to support sleep processes. You can also try adding flaxseeds in your morning smoothie or oatmeal, which is an easy way to incorporate them into your diet.

The Effects of a Poor Diet

On the flip side, a diet high in processed foods negatively impacts sleep quality. Processed foods often contain additives and high levels of sugar, which can disrupt the balance of neurotransmitters in the brain. For example, studies have shown that consuming high amounts of sugar can lead to spikes in energy followed by crashes that may keep a person awake. This cycle can prevent the body from achieving the deeper stages of sleep. Reducing processed foods and maintaining a diet rich in whole foods can go a long way in improving overall sleep.

Why Whole Foods Matter

Whole foods are those that are minimally processed and close to their natural state. These foods provide more vitamins, minerals, and other nutrients that the body needs. Eating whole foods leads to a better nutritional profile that supports many bodily functions, including sleep. For example, whole grains like brown rice and quinoa not only provide energy but also help in producing serotonin. Incorporating these grains into meals can keep you satisfied and help set the stage for a restful night.

Building a Sleep-Conducive Diet

To foster better sleep, it is essential to build meals around these nutritious foods. Begin by planning your meals for the week. Include items like lean proteins, whole grains, vegetables, and healthy fats. At breakfast, opt for oatmeal topped with nuts and fruits. For lunch, try a salad loaded with veggies and beans, and for dinner, include fish or chicken with a side of sweet potatoes and steamed greens. Snacks can consist of yogurt with seeds or a piece of fruit.

Timing Your Meals

In addition to choosing the right foods, timing your meals can make a big difference for your sleep. Eating a large meal right before bed can lead to discomfort and disrupted sleep. It's generally recommended to finish eating at least a few hours before bedtime. This gives your body time to digest. If you need a snack closer to bedtime, choose something light, such as a banana or a small bowl of almonds.

Staying Hydrated

Hydration plays a crucial role in sleep. Maintaining proper fluid levels throughout the day ensures that the body functions optimally, affecting everything from metabolism to energy levels. However, timing is key. Consuming too much liquid close to bedtime can disrupt sleep with frequent bathroom visits. Limiting fluid intake in the evening—particularly diuretic beverages like coffee, tea, and alcohol—helps maintain sleep continuity. These beverages can amplify the body's need to urinate, fragmenting deep sleep phases. Optimal hydration practices involve consistent fluid consumption throughout the day but tapering off as bedtime approaches, preventing disruptive awakenings and encouraging more restful sleep.

The Relationship Between Nutrition and Sleep

Understanding the connection between food and sleep helps highlight the importance of making informed dietary choices. As we have seen, nutrient-rich foods promote better sleep by boosting the body's ability to produce essential sleep-related neurotransmitters. Conversely, processed foods can hinder sleep by disrupting neurotransmitter balance. Being mindful of what we eat can positively impact how well we rest at night.

More Details on Encouraging Better Eating Habits

To encourage better eating habits, consider keeping a food journal. Write down everything you eat and how you feel after each meal. This can help identify which foods contribute to good sleep and which ones might disrupt it. You can also share your journey with friends or family for accountability. Their support can motivate you to stick to a diet that favors sleep.

By making simple dietary changes and being aware of how food affects sleep, you can create habits that lead to improved rest and overall well-being. As you incorporate more leafy greens, nuts, and seeds into your diet and reduce processed foods, you may begin to notice the positive changes in your sleep patterns and overall health..

Meal timing and portion sizes play a significant role in sleep onset and duration. Eating large meals late at night often hinders sleep initiation because the body stays active processing the meal rather than preparing for rest. The physical discomfort from large portions can disrupt sleep cycles by extending sleep-onset latency, the time taken to fall asleep.

Instead, maintaining regular meal times helps stabilize the sleep-wake cycle, allowing the body to follow a predictable rhythm (St-Onge et al., 2016). Ideally, finishing meals two to three hours before bedtime allows digestion to occur before sleep. Incorporating smaller, balanced meals spread throughout the day rather than concentrating heavy meals in the evening eases the body into restful sleep. Breakfast, highly prioritized for its impact on metabolism, should remain regular to set a functional daily rhythm that supports effective sleep patterns.

Understanding your own meal timing preferences is another crucial aspect of optimizing sleep. Everyone's digestive system and metabolism operate on slightly different schedules, meaning what works for one person may not work for another. Exploring these individual preferences and aligning meal timings with personal sleep needs can foster a more harmonious relationship with sleep patterns. Pay attention to how different meal times affect your sleep quality and adjust your routine accordingly.

Specific food combinations also hold potential to promote better sleep outcomes. Pairing carbohydrates with protein facilitates sleep through its influence on serotonin and melatonin production. Carbohydrates aid the brain's uptake of tryptophan, a precursor to serotonin, thus promoting sleepiness and enhancing sleep quality. Effective combinations might include whole-grain bread with turkey slices or oatmeal with almonds, providing both the tryptophan and the carbohydrate needed to optimize tryptophan absorption. The increase in serotonin levels subsequently assists in melatonin production, further promoting sleep readiness (St-Onge et al., 2016; Sejbuk et al., 2022).

Epidemiological findings further support dietary influences on sleep. A cross-sectional study indicated that diets high in confectionery and noodles are associated with poor sleep quality, evidenced by higher Pittsburgh Sleep Quality Index scores. In contrast, fish and vegetable-rich diets correlate with improved sleep quality (St-Onge et al., 2016). An excess of carbohydrates, especially poor-quality ones from processed foods, emerged as a significant factor in sleep disruptions. Such dietary patterns might even prompt larger sleep problems that disrupt overall health.

In considering macronutrient interactions, Tanaka et al. (2016) revealed that low protein intake links with sleep difficulties, highlighting the balance needed in protein consumption to maintain hormonal balance crucial for sleep. Insufficient carbohydrates, too, relate to disordered sleep patterns, reflecting how dietary imbalances affect sleep quality. Moreover, diet impacts are often sex-specific; in some cases, men show different susceptibilities to dietary influences on sleep compared to women (St-Onge et al., 2016).

Adopting a Mediterranean diet pattern laden with fruits, vegetables, nuts, and whole grains connects with better sleep outcomes, especially in older adults, illustrating how comprehensive dietary shifts aid sleep. This particular diet supports not just sleep, but an overall healthier lifestyle that in turn impacts sleep quality positively. However, as data indicates, some effects like the inverse association between such a diet and insomnia symptoms appear more pronounced in women (St-Onge et al., 2016).

The discussed dietary influences underscore that broader dietary patterns, not just isolated food choices, culminate in the quality and duration of sleep. Recognizing the roles these various dietary elements play helps individuals tailor their eating habits to support sleep health optimally. Maintaining steady, nutrient-rich diets, along with consciously regulating food intake timing and hydration, promotes a holistic approach to better sleep practices. In doing so, individuals struggling with sleep issues can see marked improvements in both sleep quality and overall well-being.

As we transition into examining specific elements like carbohydrates and chocolate on sleep, we will delve deeper into the distinctions between simple and complex carbs and discuss chocolate's unique impact, further illuminating dietary nuances that affect sleep. This segue sets the stage to further dissect how particular food categories interconnect with sleep and guide precise dietary adjustments beneficial for sleep enhancement.

Carbs and Chocolate Effects

As we've seen how nutrient-dense meals and timing affect sleep, choosing the right carbohydrates can also enhance your rest. It's not just about eating carbohydrates, but understanding their type and impact on sleep. Simple carbohydrates, like those found in sugary snacks or white bread, can lead to quick surges in blood sugar followed by sharp drops, causing energy crashes that disrupt sleep. Imagine snacking on a donut before bed and finding yourself tossing and turning shortly after.

On the other hand, complex carbohydrates, such as whole grains and legumes, offer a more stable release of energy, supporting smoother transitions into sleep. Swapping out a sugary evening snack for a bowl of oatmeal or some chickpea salad can make a noticeable difference in how you wind down at night. These foods don't just stabilize blood sugar levels; they also trigger the release of serotonin, a hormone linked to mood and sleep quality. This hormone release aids in relaxing your body, paving the way for better sleep quality (Sejbuk et al., 2022).

Now, moving on to chocolate, many view it as a nighttime indulgence without realizing its effects on sleep. Chocolate contains caffeine, with dark chocolate having more than its milk counterpart. This caffeine can interfere with your ability to fall and stay asleep. A couple of squares of dark chocolate might perk you up when you should be unwinding, leading to restless nights or even difficulty maintaining sleep. Therefore, while that late-night chocolate fix might seem harmless, it's essential to keep its caffeine content in mind when seeking restful sleep. (Personal Note: I am the type of person that needs something sweet after very meal. Normally, I was ending my meal with a Lindt white chocolate ball, but I have now graduated to fruit, like strawberries of raspberries. Yes, I do miss my Lindt, but switching to a more natural sugar has helped my sleep. But I still do keep Lindt balls in the house, just in case.)

However, chocolate isn't all bad news when it comes to sleep. Some types contain compounds like theobromine, which can promote relaxation and even sleepiness in small doses. It's a delicate balance, as too much chocolate can still lead to disrupted sleep due to its sugar content and stimulants. If you MUST have choclate (and I do understand), opt for varieties with lower sugar and caffeine content, like milk chocolate or perhaps a small serving of the aforementioned white chocolate, if you're looking to satisfy that sweet tooth without comprising your sleep.

Moreover, it's crucial to distinguish between craving and hunger, particularly in the context of nighttime snacking. Emotional or stress-induced cravings for carbs and chocolate can lead to poor eating habits, disrupting your sleep. Picture coming home late, feeling stressed, and reaching for a bag of chips or a chocolate bar to unwind. This pattern can easily become a cycle if not managed.

To tackle these cravings, try developing mindful snacking habits. Identify your triggers—are you truly hungry, or is that chocolate bar calling because you're feeling anxious or bored? Recognize these patterns and replace them with healthier alternatives that were mentioned, like a few nuts or fruit. And importantly, establish a nighttime routine that helps you avoid junk food pitfalls, such as setting a no-snack time an hour before bed (Sejbuk et al., 2022).

A big part of our relationship with carbs and chocolate involves their personality as comfort foods. Think back to childhood memories of eating cookies and feeling cozy, or how the smell of freshly baked bread sends waves of nostalgia and comfort. These emotional connections can drive your food choices and influence your sleep cycles. If indulging in a chocolate cookie before bed is tied to relaxation in your mind, it might be hard to see this habit as disruptive to sleep, even if it is. Currently my favorite dessert is Tiramisu, but if the ladyfinger cookies in the dessert have been soaked in coffee or espresso, and then the dessert is topped with cocoa, then I cannot order for fear of knowing I will not sleep. Therefore, when ordering a nice dessert at a restaurant, I unfortunately often choose something light without chocolate or caffeine. (Note: When making Tiramisu at home, try using decaf coffee!)

Reframing ones mindset about these foods can make a significant impact. Next time you're craving something, ask yourself if it's nourishing to your body and whether it contributes to a restful night's sleep. Focus on creating positive associations with foods that can support your health holistically. Choose to see carbs and chocolate not as barriers to sleep but as parts of a balanced diet that could coexist with your sleep goals in moderation.

Finally, let's link this discussion to understanding caffeine's pivotal role in the sleep equation. Just as the right carbs and mindful chocolate consumption can improve sleep patterns, moderating caffeine intake is another crucial piece of the puzzle. While caffeine can offer a much-needed jolt during the day, it also plays a significant role in affecting your sleep duration and quality. The interplay of caffeine, carbohydrates, and chocolate consumption is delicate, and balancing these elements in your diet can provide deeper insights into achieving restorative sleep. As we continue the exploration into dietary factors impacting sleep, examining how caffeine fits into this landscape will paint a broader picture of how your daily intakes work together to shape your nights (Sejbuk et al., 2022).

The Role of Caffeine in Sleep

Caffeine significantly impacts sleep quality and duration in various ways. To understand this impact, one must first consider how the body metabolizes caffeine and its half-life. Caffeine has a half-life of about 3 to 7 hours, which means it takes this long for half of it to be eliminated from the body. This extended presence in the system can alter later sleep stages, particularly REM sleep, which plays a crucial role in mood regulation and cognitive functions (Rodak et al., 2021). The longer caffeine remains in the bloodstream, the more it disrupts sleep cycles, leading to fragmented sleep or difficulty entering deeper, restorative stages of sleep.

For those more sensitive to caffeine's effects, timing of consumption becomes especially significant. Consuming caffeine in the afternoon or evening can lead to insufficient sleep by delaying sleep onset or decreasing sleep duration (Drake et al., 2013). Studies show that even caffeine taken 6 hours before bedtime can disrupt sleep architecture (Drake et al.,

2013). (Personally, I do not have any caffeine or chocolate after 12:00 noon, which I have notice has been helping my sleep.) Drake's evidence underscores the importance of regulating caffeine intake, particularly in the latter part of the day. Reducing caffeine consumption or abstaining from caffeine eight hours before bed can significantly improve sleep outcomes for those who experience sleep disruptions linked to caffeine.

Hidden sources of caffeine often contribute to unintentional overconsumption, affecting sleep. Beyond coffee and energy drinks, caffeine lurks in sodas, teas, chocolate, and certain medications. Unawareness of these hidden sources can lead to higher caffeine intake than intended. Learning to read food and drink labels is crucial for managing total caffeine consumption effectively. By becoming more aware of these hidden sources, individuals can adopt sleep-friendly dietary habits, minimizing inadvertent sleep disturbances.

Another layer in understanding caffeine's influence on sleep involves individual differences in caffeine tolerance. Some people metabolize caffeine more quickly due to genetic factors, allowing them to drink it later in the day without impacting their sleep significantly (Rodak et al., 2021). Conversely, others may find their sleep interrupted even with moderate caffeine intake earlier in the day. Recognizing these tolerance differences helps individuals make informed decisions about their caffeine consumption. Trying a reduction in caffeine intake can be enlightening; observing changes in sleep patterns can provide tangible evidence of caffeine's effects.

One thing to bring-up ion this section is the difference between *synthetic caffeine* and *natural caffeine* and how they differ primarily in their sources and composition. Natural caffeine is derived from plants like coffee beans, tea leaves, and cacao pods, while synthetic caffeine is chemically manufactured in a lab, often used in energy drinks and supplements. The body metabolizes these two forms differently; natural caffeine comes with other beneficial compounds such as antioxidants, which may moderate its effects. Natural caffeine generally releases more slowly into the system due to the presence of other compounds, potentially leading to fewer disruptions in sleep patterns. In contrast, synthetic caffeine, being a concentrated and isolated form, may lead to a quicker spike in energy levels, which could increase the likelihood of insomnia or disrupted sleep, especially when consumed later in the day. Understanding these differences can help individuals make informed choices regarding their caffeine consumption and its impact on sleep quality.

As we know, a person's mood is intricately tied to their sleep quality... and is further influenced by caffeine. High caffeine consumption can exacerbate feelings of anxiety and stress (Rodak et al., 2021). During the night, increased anxiety levels translate to restless or shallow sleep, creating a vicious cycle where poor sleep exacerbates anxiety, which in turn disrupts sleep further. Lowering caffeine intake often leads to noticeable improvements in mood stability and sleep quality. Managing caffeine helps stabilize mood, creating a positive feedback loop, enhancing both emotional well-being and sleep.

The individual response to caffeine reduction varies, emphasizing the need for personal experimentation. By gradually decreasing intake or eliminating it entirely, individuals can experience improved sleep and mood over time. Tracking sleep quality and mood changes offers practical insights into caffeine's role in each individual's nightly rest. This self-awareness aids in crafting a more personalized approach to consuming this common stimulant while fostering healthier sleep habits.

Approaching dietary modifications related to caffeine should include considerations for how caffeine intersects with personal lifestyle and health goals. Some may choose to forego caffeine due to its disruptive potential, while others might simply adjust timing and quantity to align with a need for optimal function. Understanding one's relationship with caffeine allows for more strategic consumption, integrating this awareness into broader dietary and sleep hygiene practices.

This exploration of caffeine and its effects on sleep quality naturally leads to other dietary factors influencing sleep, such as carbohydrates and fats. As this discussion progresses, the focus will shift to examining how alcohol consumption affects sleep. Understanding the compounds within various alcoholic beverages and their influence on sleep cycles can further enlighten a holistic approach to optimizing sleep quality through dietary adjustments. Tracking how different dietary components impact sleep can empower individuals to form more targeted strategies in enhancing their overall well-being.

Influence of Alcohol, Wine, and Beer

Alcohol, like caffeine, profoundly affects our sleep architecture. Caffeine's ability to keep us alert is widely recognized, but we should similarly consider alcohol's impact on our sleep patterns. Both substances disrupt our sleep, becoming a critical factor to contemplate for anyone seeking to improve their sleep quality. Let's dive into how alcohol disturbs our restful state and why moderating its consumption could be crucial for better sleep.

Alcohol presents a significant challenge to maintaining restorative sleep due to its effects on REM sleep. Typically, individuals cycle through various sleep stages, including REM, essential for memory consolidation and mood regulation. Alcohol tends to shorten REM duration, leading to a less restorative sleep experience (Roehrs & Roth, 2024). This disruption often results in feelings of fatigue and diminished cognitive performance the following day.

Consuming alcohol close to bedtime may initially seem beneficial due to its sedative properties, which can hasten sleep onset. However, this initial benefit is misleading. Over the night, as alcohol metabolizes, sleep becomes fragmented. In fact, increased wake times and lighter sleep phases often occur in the latter part of the night, a phenomenon coined the "rebound effect" (Roehrs & Roth, 2024). This disrupted pattern significantly hinders achieving the deep restorative sleep necessary for optimal daily functioning.

Shifting habits to limit alcohol intake could yield impressive sleep quality improvements. Reducing consumption can make sleep more continuous and less disrupted, reflecting a more typical sleep cycle pattern. This change enhances both sleep quality and duration, thereby promoting improved mood, energy levels, and mental clarity.

Notably, while alcohol as a whole affects sleep, different alcoholic beverages have distinct impacts. Beer, for instance, can lead to bloating due to its carbonation, leading to physical discomfort during sleep. This discomfort can interrupt sleeping patterns by prompting awakenings throughout the night. On the other hand, wine, particularly sweet varieties, concerns itself with sugar content, potentially affecting blood sugar levels. Fluctuating glucose levels may disrupt sleep cycles, contributing to fragmented rest. Although you may think you got a full night's rest, in reality your cycles have been interrupted.

When assessing how alcohol influences your sleep patterns, take note of the type of alcohol you drink and the different effects it has on your sleep. Personally, red wine is like drinking an Energy Drink for me, and will keep me awake the entire night. While, have a beer or two has a less effect.

It's crucial to debunk the myth that alcohol helps with relaxation and, consequently, sleep. The initial calming sensation is short-lived and deceptive. Post-consumption, the body experiences disrupted REM stages and increased awakenings, which counters the true need for relaxation during sleep. Clear understanding and mindful consumption choices play an essential role in ensuring that relaxation is genuine, especially during sleep.

A plethora of healthier, non-alcoholic beverage options exists for those looking to improve their sleep. By substituting alcohol with these alternatives—such as (less fun) herbal teas or water—before bedtime, individuals can avoid the sleep disruptions associated with alcohol. Warm chamomile tea, for instance, serves as an excellent relaxing substitute without the adverse effects on sleep architecture.

Alcohol consumption often intertwines with cultural and social influences, making it a staple in numerous social situations. This social pressure can lead to regular or excessive alcohol consumption without considering its detrimental impact on sleep. Cultivating mindfulness in social settings involves being conscious of alcohol intake choices and understanding how such moments could impact sleep later on. (This has been one of my biggest challenges.) By being proactive, individuals can balance social participation while ensuring sufficient rest, consequently improving their health overall.

Understanding the role of alcohol within the dietary influences on sleep chapter highlights its multifaceted impact. We explored how it disrupts sleep architecture, highlights among different beverages, and substitutes oneself with healthier alternatives. These insights empower readers to make informed choices, considering both personal well-being and the potential societal expectations surrounding alcohol consumption.

Concrete examples and deeper explanations are essential. For instance, those who regularly consume alcohol might find their sleep quality significantly improves even with modest reductions in intake. Such examples enable readers to understand the nuanced relationship between alcohol and sleep clearly. Each individual's experience with alcohol and sleep will vary, emphasizing the importance of personalized moderation.

Repetition and redundant statements detract from this narrative, necessitating concise, precise writing. By maintaining focus on the core theme—alcohol's impact on sleep—we provide a coherent and informative narrative without unnecessary diversions. Similarly, avoiding participle phrases throughout ensures clarity by allowing the section to flow naturally with a clear line of argument.

By addressing the misconceptions about alcohol and providing strategies for healthier alternatives, this section offers actionable advice. This information lays the groundwork for readers to reflect on their consumption habits and make decisions that align with their health goals. Ultimately, moderation serves not only to enhance sleep but also to promote better physical and mental well-being.

In conclusion, understanding alcohol's impact on sleep establishes a crucial step in the pursuit of improved sleep quality. By being aware of how different types of alcohol affect sleep and considering alternatives, individuals can more effectively manage their intake and create optimal resting conditions. Such strategic lifestyle changes not only optimize sleep quality but also extend to broader aspects of health and well-being.

Concluding Thoughts

Understanding the intricate connection between diet and sleep sheds light on the path to better rest and overall well-being. This exploration reveals that the right mix of nutrients, balanced food choices, and strategic meal timing can significantly enhance sleep quality. By opting for nutrient-dense foods, moderating carbohydrate intake, and watching caffeine and alcohol consumption, we provide our bodies with tools to journey towards sounder sleep. As we delve into dietary specifics like carbohydrates and chocolate, a more profound understanding emerges about how small changes in food habits can lead to significant improvements in sleep health. Now equipped with this knowledge, you can tailor your nutrition to align with your sleep goals, paving the way for deeper rest and improved vitality.

Chapter 6

Environmental Impact on Sleep Quality

Have you ever found yourself tossing and turning in bed, unable to fall asleep despite the late hour? Maybe it happens every night as you lie there, wide awake, your mind buzzing like a neon sign. You try everything—from counting those dumb-ass sheep to practicing deep breathing—but nothing seems to work. Could it be something in your environment that's sabotaging your sleep?

The connection between our surroundings and sleep quality is an intriguing one that many overlook. From the glow of streetlights creeping through the curtains to the persistent hum of electronic devices, these environmental factors can significantly disturb our natural sleep patterns. In this chapter, we'll explore how your environment might be impacting your rest and what changes could help steer you towards more restful nights.

Technology and Lighting Effects

Although the topic of Technology has it's own chapter in this book (Chapter 9), I wanted to lightly touch upon this theme, since technology is a part of our environment. The impact of artificial light on our sleep cycle demonstrates the complexity of modern life interfacing with human biology. Technology, once a dawn-to-dusk utility, now illuminates our nights, altering biological signals that govern sleep. Studies have identified a significant link between artificial light at night (ALAN) and the suppression of melatonin, a hormone indispensable for initiating sleep. Melatonin production diminishes sharply when exposed to blue light emanating from screens and LED bulbs. Modern electronics, with their prevalence of high-intensity light, exacerbate this problem. Implementing changes such as substituting cool, intense light sources with warm-toned alternatives can significantly help. This kind of lighting conducive to relaxation encourages natural melatonin production, suggesting that eliminating blue light exposure before bed could substantially improve sleep onset (Davis et al., 2023).

Smart devices, omnipresent around the clock, extend technological interference beyond physical lighting to digital engagement. Smartphones, tablets, and laptops continue to emit blue light, often wielded late into the night. This continual bombardment of light cues keeps our bodies alert, a physiological behavior misaligned with our natural circadian rhythms. To mitigate these effects, limiting device use in the hour preceding sleep can be advantageous. Although many smart devices have setting that can lower brightness, or create a "true tone", alternatives should be geared toward relaxation rather than stimulation, such as reading a book or practicing mindfulness techniques.

A nuanced aspect to consider is lighting temperature's role in alertness and relaxation. Blue light, often produced by LEDs, energizes and enhances focus, suited for daytime tasks. Switching to dim, warm-toned lights (as mentioned above) in the evening can encourage a sense of calmness, signaling to our bodies that it's time to wind down. Adjusting these lights gradually reflects the natural, decreasing sunlight exposure, aligning closely with biological expectations.

Night mode features, increasingly prevalent on devices, provide a practical response to blue light exposure. Reducing screen emission's intensity and warmth, these settings help in transitioning into rest. Scheduling a consistent activation of night mode can favorably impact sleep quality, nudging our cheat-laden rhythms back towards nature-aligned patterns (Davis et al., 2023).

Emerging research highlights the substantial effect of circadian rhythm disruptions arising from non-natural lighting evolution. Anthropologically, humans synchronized with dawn and dusk, a balance disrupted post-industrialization. With digital screens today offering intense doses of artificial light, circadian misalignments manifest in delayed sleep and fragmented cycles. These adjustments, however slight, can elevate risks associated with numerous health issues, including insomnia and mood fluctuations (Duan et al., 2024).

A significant study conducted in 2024 across various cities in mainland China highlights the growing concerns regarding artificial light at night (ALAN). This study is important because it sheds light on how increased exposure to artificial light during nighttime is linked to higher rates of insomnia. Insomnia is a condition where individuals find it difficult to fall or stay asleep, which can lead to various health problems. The researchers utilized a combination of social media data and nighttime satellite imagery to gather their findings. This approach allowed them to analyze patterns of light exposure in different areas and how these patterns relate to the sleep health of residents.

As the study reveals, there is a clear correlation between the amount of artificial light people are exposed to at night and the frequency of sleep disturbances they experience. For instance, in cities where streetlights are brighter and more numerous, residents reported higher incidences of insomnia. The research indicated that as exposure to artificial light increased, the rates of sleep disturbances also rose. This information suggests that the environment we live in can significantly influence our sleep quality. The study's findings are particularly alarming because they extend our understanding of health issues that arise from living in a digitally illuminated age. It's not just about how well we sleep; it also connects to broader health concerns that can arise from poor sleep quality. (Duan et al., 2024).

The ripple effects of digital engagement and artificial lighting necessitate actionable solutions. Establishing a bedroom environment conducive to healthy sleep, informed by awareness of these influences, becomes imperative. Concrete steps such as turning off electronics after a certain hour, ensuring curtains prevent outdoor light bleed, and preferring ambient, warm-toned lights redefine sleep spaces. These adjustments extend into daily routines, urging mechanical regularity in sleep timing and supported relaxation activities.

This exploration transitions organically into understanding the physical design of sleep environments. Beyond light sources, how one's room is structured holds pivotal importance. Optimal bed placement, avoidance of clutter, and mastering room temperature establish an atmosphere inviting to uninterrupted sleep. The upcoming discussion will examine how these physical elements integrate with light management for enhancing restorative sleep. Together, these components offer a layered strategy for improving sleep quality in the face of constant technological and environmental stimuli.

Hence, managing our artificial light exposure translates directly into effective sleep strategies. It involves distinguishing between when light serves as a needed cue for alertness and when it's an avoidable interference. This definitive awareness drives practical adjustments. Embedding prudent habits like retreating from screens well before bed, orchestrating calming pre-sleep rituals, and maintaining thoughtfully designed environments can dramatically enhance sleep quality amidst technological prevalence. These nuanced narratives of cause and effect navigate the reader towards resolving sleep-related challenges within modern contexts, ensuring the content remains direct and solution-oriented.

Optimal Bedroom Design

As we explore the journey towards creating an optimal sleep environment, it's clear that physical bedroom design complements the technological and lighting adjustments previously discussed. This synergy ensures a holistic environment that promotes rest and rejuvenation. As we've seen, the interplay between technology use and lighting can significantly influence sleep quality. Equally essential is the bedroom's offerings (pillows, blankets, bedding) and the actual physical layout of the room , which supports these aspects by minimizing disruptions and maximizing comfort.

The quality of bed and pillow plays a crucial role in determining the overall quality of sleep. A well-constructed mattress provides the necessary support for the spine, ensuring proper alignment and reducing the risk of back pain. Similarly, a high-quality pillow can greatly affect neck alignment and comfort, preventing discomfort that can disrupt sleep. Sleep studies have shown that individuals who invest in quality bedding often experience deeper and more restorative sleep cycles. Additionally, poor quality beds and pillows can lead to tossing and turning throughout the night, depriving the body of essential rest. Overall, investing in quality sleep essentials is vital for enhancing sleep quality and promoting better health and well-being.

When discussing bed orientation and placement, think first about tranquility. Placing the bed away from windows, hallways, or other noise sources can drastically reduce disturbances. This setup is particularly relevant when considering how ambient conditions, like sound, impact sleep quality (Buonanno et al., 2024). A comfortable mattress tailored to personal preference can enhance relaxation and posture, reducing pressure points and promoting uninterrupted sleep. Custom bedding, whether it includes weighted blankets or cooling sheets, can provide additional layers of comfort, catering to the sensory needs of the sleeper.

Temperature control in the bedroom is another critical factor in achieving quality sleep. The ideal room temperature lies within a cool range, often cited as between 15.6 and 19.4 degrees Celsius (60 - 67 degrees fahrenheit), supporting the body's natural temperature drop during sleep (Emmitt, 2023). Fans or HVAC systems can regulate temperatures, adapting to seasonal changes. For those without air conditioning, simple adjustments like layering blankets can help maintain body heat in winter and allow easy removal for cooling in summer.

Clutter in the bedroom can lead to a mental landscape equally disordered, hindering rest. A clutter-free environment reduces stress and the chances of sleep disturbance, as indicated by the ambient conditions necessary for high sleep quality (Buonanno et al., 2024). Employing a minimalistic design aids in creating a sanctuary free from distraction, where every item has its place. Built-in storage solutions can help maintain tidiness and streamline bedroom processes, allowing the bedroom to remain a place of rest rather than a chaotic environment. Also, allowing for a clutter-free bedroom will help with dust build-up on items which could affect your sleeping and allergic reactions.

Soundproofing becomes invaluable in urban settings or homes with thin walls where external noise is inevitable. Techniques such as installing heavier drapes, using soundproofing curtains, or even sound-absorbing panels can shield the bedroom from unwanted sounds. In addition to the sound masking in your sleeping environment, is the visual enhancements that can be added to the bedroom. One trick that I use is a child's ceiling projector. This toy-nightlight projects stars and slow a moving galaxy light affects onto my bedroom ceiling. This calming tactic signals to my brain, that it is time to begin to relax.

Notably, the effectiveness of these strategies is underscored by their inter-connectedness. The cumulative effect of proper bed placement, maintained temperature, an orderly environment, and sound management forms a cohesive picture of how physical changes promote better sleep (Emmitt, 2023). This synergy mirrors physiological processes essential for restorative sleep, helping regulate heart rate and respiratory patterns, which are vital for health, as identified in field studies (Buonanno et al., 2024).

By embracing a holistic approach that combines these physical environment adjustments with previous insights on technology and lighting, you can create a conducive atmosphere that significantly enhances sleep quality. This balanced approach not only mitigates adverse environmental factors but also aligns with natural sleep rhythms, laying the foundation for well-being and health. The interconnectedness of these factors reinforces the complexity of sleep and the myriad ways in which our immediate environment contributes to its quality. Understanding this allows for a carefully tailored sleeping environment that caters to individual needs, promoting better nights and, consequently, better days.

Colour Schemes for Better Sleep

As we segue into the topic of colour schemes, consider how this transition not only signals a shift but also highlights an essential component of bedroom design. Having a formal background in design, I enjoy focusing on how colours play a profound role in shaping psychological and physiological states. Certain hues can elicit calmness and relaxation, further enhancing sleep quality. Blue or green tones, known for their soothing properties, can transform a bedroom into an oasis of restfulness, setting the stage for sleep even before the lights dim. This colour strategy will pave the way for deeper exploration into how psychological factors interact with bedroom aesthetics to influence sleep, an area we'll explore next.

Colour in the bedroom, much like room arrangement and minimalistic design principles, significantly influences sleep quality. The right colour choice can enhance the serene atmosphere needed for restful nights, reinforcing previously mentioned design strategies that focus on the physical layout of the room, such as keeping clutter to a minimum to create a distraction-free sleep haven.

Colours wield the power to evoke varied emotional responses. Blues and greens, often synonymous with serenity and calm, demonstrate this effect vividly. According to bedroom colour psychology, these hues mimic the tranquility of ocean waves or the peaceful embrace of lush forests, signaling your brain that it's time to relax, subsequently lowering heart rate and blood pressure (Homemakers Furniture, 2024). These colours accomplish more than just visual appeal; they help create a state of relaxation that primes the body for quality sleep. In contrast, stimulating colours like red and orange can energize and disrupt sleep patterns. Thus, understanding these psychological effects allows for strategic colour choices in the bedroom, fostering an environment that supports relaxation and rest.

When choosing colours, the aim is to curate a personal space that not only appeals aesthetically but also delivers psychological benefits. Textiles, paint, and décor should harmonize to enhance mood and facilitate better sleep. Soft whites, creams, and lavenders offer a gentle, comforting palette that envelops you in a secure and tranquil atmosphere, promoting a peaceful transition from wakefulness to slumber (Homemakers Furniture, 2024). The use of these colours in bedding or curtains can soften the room's overall feel, ensuring that the mind is gently eased into rest.

Introducing earthy tones like sage green and terracotta can ground the bedroom environment, connecting it to nature and promoting feelings of stability. These hues are particularly beneficial for quieting a restless mind, creating a cocoon-like effect that aids in deep relaxation (Homemakers Furniture, 2024). Meanwhile, colours like soft pinks and grays, while seemingly unconventional, can also foster a calming atmosphere when used thoughtfully. Imagine a dusty rose blush or a calming dove-gray wall; these colours invite a sense of tranquility without overpowering a room. The strategic use of colour can revitalize a room, supporting peaceful sleep while reflecting individual tastes.

In crafting the perfect colour palette, remember the role of lighting. The interplay between colour and lighting shapes the bedroom's overall atmosphere. For example, a soft yellow light can accentuate the warmth of lavender walls, while a cool white light might enhance the freshness of sage green, influencing how these colours affect the mood (Summer, 2023). The goal is to create harmony between colour and light, ensuring the bedroom remains a sanctuary for restfulness rather than stimulation.

Concrete examples further illustrate the importance of strategic colour choices. For instance, a room with pale blue walls can pair beautifully with crisp white linens and touches of greenery, like a potted plant. This combination can evoke the serenity of a clear day at the beach, mentally transporting you to a more relaxed state. On the other hand, a black feature wall alongside soft gray furnishings might add depth and sophistication, creating a modern haven that's as restful as it is stylish. Each colour choice can layer in different dimensions of calm, reinforcing relaxation without overwhelming the senses.

Neutral tones like beige, taupe, and soft grays serve as a versatile backdrop for bolder accent colours, allowing creativity without disrupting tranquility (Homemakers Furniture, 2024). The use of accent colours is where personal taste aligns with the psychological impact of colour. A pop of turquoise in pillows or throws can invigorate a predominantly neutral room, adding life without introducing chaos. Such mindful applications of colour enable a customized space tailored to individual sleep needs.

For practical application, consider incorporating colour palettes that adhere to these principles in textiles like sheets, blankets, and rugs. Layering different textures can add depth and richness, further promoting a relaxing atmosphere. Use a variety of fabric materials such as cotton, linen, or wool, which not only contribute to aesthetic variation but also offer comfort. A cashmere throw over a linen bedspread, for instance, adds an embracing warmth that complements calming colours.

By structuring this section to introduce new concepts progressively, we steer clear of redundancy, ensuring that each idea builds upon the last. Discussing how colours affect mood seamlessly leads to exploring practical design choices, keeping the narrative engaging and informative without rehashing points.

Ending on the note that just as colour can alter mood and promote better sleep, so too can other environmental factors like fragrances and ambient noise, sets the stage for our next exploration. Scented candles or essential oil diffusers can introduce calming aromas that complement the visual serenity of a well-chosen colour palette. Similarly, soundscapes help tune out disturbances, inviting deeper rest. The upcoming section will delve into how combining these elements can forge an optimal sleep environment, uniting the influences of sight, smell, and sound into a cohesive nocturnal retreat.

Fragrances and Ambient Noise

As we continue our exploration of sleep environments, let's pivot from colours to scents and ambient noise, both significant players in creating restful atmospheres. Unlike colours, which we see and directly tie to emotional responses, scents and sounds envelop us subtly, influencing our states of relaxation and alertness almost imperceptibly. This sensory overlap encourages us to think about sleep spaces more holistically, recognizing that a room's serenity extends beyond what we see to include what we smell and hear.

The influence of fragrances on sleep is profound yet personal. The basics of aromatherapy explain how scents like lavender and jasmine have long been associated with relaxation and calming effects, which is vital for those seeking rest at night (Sabiniewicz et al., 2022). This isn't mere folklore—lavender's properties have been shown to increase total sleep time and enhance sleep effectiveness among various populations, including those with insomnia (Sabiniewicz et al., 2022). When choosing fragrances, it's crucial to understand personal scent preferences, which can greatly affect how scents contribute to the sleep environment. Incorporating these scents into a regular bedtime routine can create a comforting association with sleep, a ritual that signals to the body and mind that it's time to wind down.

Moving from scent to sound, ambient noise can both mask disruptions and create a serene environment conducive to sleep. Some people find that silence can be surprisingly unsettling, leaving them more aware of their thoughts or the tiniest disturbances in their surroundings. Here, ambient noise or sound machines come into play. They function by drowning out sudden noises that might interrupt sleep or by creating a consistent sound backdrop that soothes the mind. Nature sounds, like rain, ocean waves, or gentle breezes, are particularly popular because they have a calming effect, reminiscent of more peaceful, natural settings.

Curated playlists of ambient sounds can offer similar comfort, shaping the auditory landscape to personal taste. The predictability of these sounds aids relaxation by occupying the mind enough to leave room for rest but not enough to engage it actively. This is where sound machines become invaluable. They offer a solution tailored to individual needs, with options ranging from white noise—which blends all frequencies of sound equally to mask disturbances—to more specialized noise, like *pink noise*, which balances frequencies more naturally to the human ear.

Selecting a sound machine that aligns with personal sleep needs can help stabilize the sleep environment. White noise machines, in particular, are prolific for promoting uninterrupted sleep. They work by creating a steady auditory stream that masks other, less consistent sounds, thus fostering a calming environment that supports longer and more restful sleep cycles. They are particularly useful in noisy urban settings or thin-walled apartments where external noises are frequent.

Noise management is another layer to consider. In spaces where external noise is unavoidable or habitual, employing soundproofing methods can make a significant difference. Simple solutions like heavy drapes, insulated windows, or draft blockers can minimize sound infiltration. Sound cushion materials, like plush rugs and padded headboards, absorb noise, contributing to a quieter bedroom. The goal is to create a sleeper-friendly sanctuary, buffered from the world's hustle and bustle outside.

Using ear plugs during sleep offers several positive qualities that can significantly enhance sleep quality. They effectively block out disruptive noises, creating a peaceful environment that promotes relaxation and allows individuals to fall asleep faster. This is particularly beneficial for those living in noisy urban areas or sharing a space with others, as ear plugs can help minimize disturbances from traffic, snoring, or late-night activities. Additionally, using ear plugs can lead to deeper and more restorative sleep by reducing the likelihood of waking up throughout the night. By ensuring a quieter atmosphere, ear plugs can ultimately contribute to improved overall health and well-being, including increased focus and heightened energy levels during the day. Personally I prefer the ear plugs made of foam that easily contour to your ear canal, however these are not environmentally friendly. Another option are the reusable silicone ear plugs (washable) which offer a eco-friendly and cost effective long term solution.

In addition to the above mentioned solutions, developing quiet habits in your wind-down routine can reinforce sleep signals. This involves dimming the lights, speaking in hushed tones, and minimizing activities that promote alertness or anxiety. The environment you cultivate before bed not only influences how quickly you fall asleep but also the quality of your rest once you do.

Bringing it all together, the interplay between scents and ambient sounds crafts an intricate, personal space ideal for sleep. It's a dance of preferences and practices, aligning with personal needs, and shaped by countless subtle decisions, from the fragrance of your pillow spray to the background hum of a noise machine. By carefully curating these elements, you can transform your bedroom into an oasis of calm, enhancing not just the quality, but the enjoyment of sleep.

Reflecting on various studies (Sabiniewicz et al., 2022; Suni, 2023), it's evident that sleep is not solely dependent on the absence of noise or the simplicity of aromatherapy but rather on how these sensory inputs align with individual preferences. This alignment is key to creating a personalized sleep haven. Fragrances must resonate with individual taste just as much as ambient sounds should soothe, underscoring the importance of trial and adaptation in designing your ideal sleep environment. The holistic approach fosters not merely rest, but a refuge from the stresses of daily life, tailored uniquely by and for you.

Concluding Thoughts

As this chapter concludes on the important role of environmental factors in sleep, it is evident that technology and biology present both challenges and opportunities. Recognizing the effects of artificial lighting, especially blue light from screens, enables us to make informed choices such as using warm-toned lights and reducing screen exposure before bedtime to enhance melatonin production. Additionally, optimizing bedroom design—covering layout and color schemes—can create an environment that promotes rest, while incorporating calming scents, sounds, and even a galaxy light show can further improve sleep quality. These practical insights allow individuals to transform their surroundings into personal spaces that support natural circadian rhythms. With this knowledge, those facing sleep issues can take concrete steps toward achieving better sleep quality, leading to deeper rest and enhanced well-being.

Chapter 7

Remedies & Medications

As someone who has battled insomnia for years, I can attest to the frustration and exhaustion that comes with trying to find the right sleeping medication. I've cycled through countless prescriptions, each promising relief but often delivering disappointment instead. The process feels like a never-ending quest, where I meticulously track my responses to each variation, hopeful that this time I'll finally get the rest I so desperately need. Each combination of medications brings its own set of side effects, and the struggle to find the perfect balance is both mentally and physically draining. The challenge of navigating this complex landscape of sleep aids often leaves me questioning not just my choices, but also the very nature of my sleep routines and well-being.

Achieving optimal sleep is a common struggle for many. In this chapter, we will examine the options available for both medication and natural remedies. These options aim to create better sleep patterns while avoiding the dreaded next-day drowsiness that can sometimes accompany them.

Understanding Medications for Sleep

Medications can effectively improve sleep, but they must be used wisely. Sleep aids fall into two categories: prescription medications, like benzodiazepines and non-benzodiazepines, which can help users fall asleep faster but carry risks of side effects and dependency, necessitating a doctor's consultation, and over-the-counter options such as diphenhydramine and melatonin, which are more accessible and generally have fewer side effects. Diphenhydramine, an antihistamine, induces drowsiness, while melatonin regulates sleep-wake cycles, particularly beneficial for those with irregular patterns. Beyond medications, there are natural remedies as well, and in the following sections we will examine choices.

Laudanum and Opium

Exploring the historic use of opium and laudanum offers a facinating glimps into how sleep-related challenges were managed in previous centuries. Laudanum emerged as a remedy with remarkable properties, particularly for inducing sleep. Historically, its use was intertwined with differing societal perceptions of drug safety and efficacy, influencing those who sought relief from sleeplessness.

Opium has a long and complex history that dates back thousands of years, primarily rooted in ancient civilizations of the Mediterranean and

Asia. The use of opium can be traced back to around 3400 BCE in Sumeria, where it was consumed for its sedative and analgesic properties. The opium poppy, Papaver somniferum, was cultivated extensively and became a significant commodity in trade. In the 19th century, opium gained immense popularity in the Western world, particularly due to the British trade in opium to China, which led to significant social and political ramifications, including the Opium Wars. This trade not only introduced opium to a broader Western audience but also resulted in widespread addiction and prompted a fierce backlash. The medicinal use of opium was endorsed by many during this time, leading to the formulation of various opiate medications, which further cemented its place in both medicine and popular culture.

The inception of laudanum (a mixture of opium and high-proof alcohol) in the 16th century marked a significant departure from prior sleep remedies. Unlike the traditional stupefactives derived from indigenous plants, laudanum's formulation combined opium and alcohol. It revolutionized the approach to sleep medicine by utilizing alchemical methods to derive therapeutic benefits while minimizing harmful effects. This change aligned with Paracelsian theories that prioritized breaking down medical compounds into safer forms. William Cecil, Lord Burghley, indirectly illustrated this importance through archival recipes, emphasizing trial and error in assessing the drug's safety and efficacy (OUP Accepted Manuscript, 2021).

As we consider the trajectory of sleep aids, it becomes essential to recognize the dichotomy between laudanum's intended calming effects and its darker potential. Prescribing laudanum became common practice for insomnia relief, particularly among the working class. This accessibility was largely due to laudanum's ability to outstrip the cost and availability of spirits, such as gin or wine (Crocq, 2007).

Laudanum's versatility enhanced its widespread acceptance, yet it also entrenched societal dependency on substance-based solutions. Its dual-purpose use for both pain relief and sedation cultivated an appeal to both medical professionals and the general public. The cultural acceptance of such remedies is deeply embedded in history. For instance, opium derivatives held a nodal role in shaping various civilizations' substance-use cultures—from Sumerians' early use of poppies to the massive addiction crisis experienced in 18th-century China (Crocq, 2007).

Beyond physical relief, laudanum had a psychological allure. Users reported a euphoric high, which contributed to its continued preference, despite known risks. The societal labeling of opium poppy and laudanum as "joy plants" was partly propagated by their celebration in myths and legends, further integrating these substances into the cultural framework of different time periods and regions. Instances of widely recounted accounts, such as Homer's tales of nepenthes, illustrate how myths propagated these drug uses through cultural literature (Crocq, 2007).

However, as 19th-century medical understanding advanced, voices from the scientific community began to challenge laudanum's and opium's unfettered use. Empirical observations and the burgeoning awareness of addiction gradually shifted perspectives from trusting the remedy to scrutinizing its adverse effects and dependency risks. The complexities of laudanum's dual nature signified a growing consciousness of its potential harms amidst its benefits. This contributed to understanding addiction as a disease, as noted by Enlightenment precepts that traced dependency not merely to weakness but also to the chemical nature of the substances themselves (Crocq, 2007).

The historical progression of laudanum and opium use underscores a transformational era in both drug understanding and public health awareness. While these substances addressed insomnia and pain, they ultimately highlighted a broader pattern of dependency that initiated pivotal debates about safety, efficacy, and ethical considerations. Within this trajectory, the collective consciousness began shifting towards a critical evaluation of relying on substance-based remedies, prompting discussions about regulated usage and the pressing demand for safer alternatives.

In effect, society's concessions about these compounds' usage revealed both a pragmatic engagement with their effects and a growing acknowledgement of their potential for abuse. Cultural perspectives varied across regions and time periods, with laudanum advancing as a cornerstone of medicinal practice. At the same time, it entailed significant burdens of side effects and dependency, contributing to a more robust societal dialogue on prevention and the need for stringent control processes.

By analyzing laudanum's and opium's trajectory, a reflection on contemporary approaches to sleep medicine becomes inevitable. The historical layer provides insights into how perceptions of dependency, therapeutic risk, and efficacy have evolved, fundamentally shaping modern attitudes towards medical treatments. The understanding of past remedies reflects a legacy of adaptation as well as discernment, driving contemporary discourse on drug safety and ethical medical practices.

Linking this comprehensive historical backdrop to modern sleep aids involves contemplating the continuity and change between old remedies and current interventions. Present-day sleep management increasingly endeavours to reconcile these histories with advanced medical knowledge and technological innovations in pharmaceuticals. The connection between both past and current approaches perpetuates a nuanced exploration into effectively balancing therapeutic benefits and dependency risks, situating sleep medicine within a broader continuum of medical progress. As we prepare to discuss contemporary medications, the stage sets up for exploring how today's options build upon and diverge from these historical antecedents, seeking holistic improvement in sleep health management.

Today's Medications

In an era far removed from the time when laudanum and opium were liberally dispensed to quiet agitated nerves or compel sleep, the landscape of sleep aids has evolved significantly. These historical remedies, once hailed for their potency, laid the foundation for today's pharmaceutical advancements in treating insomnia. The journey from these archaic beginnings to sophisticated prescription medications marks a pivotal transition in our understanding and approach to sleep disorders.

Modern prescription medications for sleep are key players in the treatment of insomnia, promising to recalibrate disrupted sleep patterns and offer relief to many who struggle with sleeplessness. They reflect a progression in medical science that intertwines biology, chemistry, and neurology to address what has become a prevalent health issue. This section aims to explore the contemporary terrain of prescribed sleep aids, shedding light on this integral component of the broader sleep treatment landscape.

Over the counter Remedies

Diphenhydramine citrate is an antihistamine commonly used as a sleep aid due to its sedative properties. (This can be found in over-the-counter medications such as Advil PM, and Zzz Quil.) It works by blocking the action of histamine, a substance in the body that plays a key role in regulating wakefulness and sleep-wake cycles. By inhibiting histamine's effects, diphenhydramine can induce feelings of drowsiness, making it easier for individuals facing insomnia or sleep disturbances to fall asleep. Moreover, its anticholinergic effects can contribute to increased relaxation and reduced nighttime arousal, thereby promoting extended periods of restful sleep.

However, while diphenhydramine citrate can provide short-term benefits for sleep, it may also have adverse effects on brain function. Some studies suggest that prolonged use can lead to cognitive impairment, especially in older adults, due to its impact on neurotransmitter systems. This can result in confusion, memory issues, and decreased alertness during waking hours. Additionally, the brain may develop a tolerance to the sedative effects over time, leading to decreased efficacy in promoting sleep. Thus, while it may serve as a temporary solution for sleep issues, caution is advised regarding its long-term use and potential cognitive effects.

Prescription Medications

Central to understanding these medications is their mechanism of action within the brain. The complex interplay of brain neurochemistry is where meds like benzodiazepines and non-benzodiazepines make their mark. They work primarily on gamma-aminobutyric acid (GABA) receptors, enhancing the effects of GABA, a neurotransmitter that dampens nerve activity to calm the nervous system (Zee et al., 2023). By augmenting GABA's inhibitory effects, these drugs induce sleep, reduce anxiety, and may even have muscle-relaxing benefits.

Generally these medications fall into two categories: benzodiazepines and Z-drugs, which are both prescription pills that help you fall asleep. Personally, I find that one's body will react better to one type than the other.

Benzodiazepines (or benzos) are depressant drugs which slow down the messages between the brain and the body. Benzos include a group of nervous system depressants prescribed for the short term treatment of stress, anxiety or insomnia. They are also known as 'minor tranquillisers' and sedatives (or sleeping pills).

Z-Drugs area class of sedative, hypnotic, and anxiolytic drugs that are used to treat insomnia and anxiety. They are also known as non-benzodiazepines because many of their names start with the letter "Z".

Benzodiazepines

- The most common type of prescription sleeping pill, but could also be prescribed as an antidepressant, or tranquilliser.

- Slow down brain and body function to help you relax and sleep

- Examples include temazepam (Restoril), loprazolam, lormetazepam, and nitrazepam, clonazepam (Klonopin)

- Recommended only for short-term use, usually less than 4 weeks

Z-drugs

- Z-drugs work similarly to benzodiazepines by binding to the GABA receptor.

- They have similar benefits, side effects, and risks to benzodiazepines.

- However, Z-drugs have different chemical structures, so they are not related to benzodiazepines on a molecular level.

- Examples include zolpidem (Ambien), eszopiclone (Lunesta), zopiclon, and zaleplon (Sonata)

- Recommended only for short-term use and can be addictive

Other types of medications that can be sleep aids include:

- Daridorexant (Quviviq), belongs to a class of drugs called *dual orexin receptor antagonists* (DORA), that works by blocking orexin receptors. The orexin signaling system regulates wakefulness, feeding, and other behaviors, and it works by blocking these receptors.

- Belsomra (Suvorexant), is also a DORA that may be better suited for those who have difficulty falling asleep.

- Antidepressants & SSRIs such as, citalopram (Celexa), escitalopram (Lexapro) mirtazepine (Remeron), trazodone, and quetiapine (Seroquel), fluoxetine (Prozac)

- Anticonvulsants, such as carbamazepine (Epitol, Tegretol -Carbatrol) and gabapentin (Neurontin)

- Tricyclic Antidepressants such as Opipramol and Doxepin, considered as a pharmacological agent (traquiliers) that does not fit the typical classification taking into account the division of antidepressants, antipsychotics and anxiolytics. Opipramol has a structure related to *tricyclic antidepressants* (doxepin) but opipramol has a slightly different mechanism of action (i.e. binding to sigma1 and to sigma2 sites). Caution is advised with possible additional treatment with neuroleptics, hypnotics and tranquillisers, but it has been report that some of these drug do not cause dependence.

You should consult a doctor before taking any medication and discuss the appropriate use, and follow all regulations. Also note that the above is not a complete listing due to the ever-changing landscape of the medical industry. These drugs can have several potential side effects, which included mental impairment, anxiety from withdrawal, and sever sedative effects, among others. Combining sleep medications with alcohol could increase the likelihood of developing adverse effects (daytime sleepiness, dizziness, headaches, changes to blood pressure, upset stomach, worsening depression, and others).

A person may find that intermittent use may help with chronic insomnia. In other words, they may find that taking it occasionally for an acute bout of insomnia may help, but they need to stop using it after a few weeks to prevent dependence.

It's crucial to distinguish the short-term from the long-term implications of these medications on sleep. In the short run, medications can be effective in recalibrating sleep cycles, helping patients fall asleep and stay asleep. Hyper-arousal is a cornerstone of insomnia that these drugs address effectively. However, long-term use is a topic rife with debate within the medical community. While some evidence supports their efficacy over months (Zee et al., 2023), concerns about dependence and diminished cognitive faculties loom large, particularly for older adults vulnerable to residual effects like dizziness and impaired motor skills (Fitzgerald & Vietri, 2015).

Efficacy and safety, especially in the context of long-term use, remain contentious. **There is no one-size-fits-all solution.** People respond variably to treatments based on genetics, lifestyle, co-existing disorders, and personal preferences. Many doctors advocate for short durations, reflecting on guidelines suggesting medications should not be used beyond three to five weeks to avoid potential harm (Zee et al., 2023). This dovetails with European guidelines echoing caution on chronic use, a stance supported by the World Sleep Society (Zee et al., 2023). Keep a sleep journal (as discussed on Chapter 3), can be useful when self-examining the affects that these individual drugs have on you personally.

Against this backdrop, it is paramount to consider the voices of those truly experiencing the effects of these aids. Testimonials and product reviews reveal a spectrum of experiences. Some praise the life-altering benefits of finally achieving restful sleep, recounting transformed mornings and renewed energy. Others report unsettling side effects, like daytime drowsiness and brain fog, which disrupt daily functions and lower the quality of life (Fitzgerald & Vietri, 2015). It is through these stories that the emotional and psychological impact of sleep medications is truly understood.

Physicians bear a hefty responsibility in this landscape, guiding patients through potential therapies and ensuring informed decisions are made. (See more about finding a medical practitioner in Chpater 11.) The consensus in medical circles stresses a <u>shared</u> decision-making model—where doctors and patients work <u>collaboratively</u>, balancing the risks and benefits specific to individual profiles (Zee et al., 2023). Herein lies the delicate art of medicine: assessing clinical guidelines against the backdrop of personal testimony.

As we consider the future of insomnia treatment, the conversation naturally shifts to embrace a more holistic viewpoint; one that integrates medications with complementary methods. This brings us to our next exploration: the role of natural remedies like herbal supplements and lifestyle adjustments, designed to work harmoniously with or in lieu of pharmaceutical interventions. By contemplating these alternatives, we pave the way for treatments that support both the body and mind, underscoring the holistic nature of healing sleep disorders.

Each component, whether pharmaceutical or natural, contributes to a tapestry of interventions aimed at combating insomnia. While medications offer significant benefits under certain circumstances, their role is ideally part of a comprehensive treatment plan. Harnessing scientific advancements while rekindling ancient wisdom offers a path forward—a convergence of worlds that promises to enhance both the quality and depth of our sleep.

Natural Remedies for Sleep

Today's sleep aids predominantly feature newer prescription medications known for their specific physiological impacts. These medications often bring immediate relief but can vary significantly in effectiveness based on individual biological responses. While these advancements offer hope for those struggling with sleep disorders, they also pave the way for an equally important exploration into natural sleep aids. Emphasizing practicality, examining the blend of traditional remedies with the latest scientific insights could yield more holistic, effective sleep solutions—not just treatments. Hildegard of Bingen (from Chapter 2) would surely approve of this.

Historically and culturally, natural remedies have always offered a treasure trove of sleep solutions. Valerian root, for example, has been used since ancient Greece for its sedative properties. It's believed to induce calmness and tranquility, a claim backed by some scientific research indicating its potential to aid in reducing the time it takes to fall asleep. Chamomile, too, boasts a rich history of use, famously consumed as a calming herbal tea across different cultures. Studies are still catching up to tradition, with research suggesting chamomile's efficacy in easing mild anxiety and promoting relaxation, thus supporting better sleep (Vora et al., 2024). Equally notable is lavender, known not only for its soothing fragrance but also for its anxiety-relieving properties. Inhaling lavender oil can calm the central nervous system, as supported by limited trials showing a significant improvement in sleep quality (Vora et al., 2024).

Melotonin

Melatonin is a hormone that is naturally produced by the pineal gland in the brain, primarily in response to darkness. It plays a crucial role in regulating the body's circadian rhythms, signaling to the body when it's time to sleep and helping to maintain a healthy sleep-wake cycle. As a supplement, melatonin can be particularly beneficial for individuals experiencing sleep disturbances, such as insomnia or jet lag. By increasing melatonin levels in the body, it can promote relaxation and a sense of drowsiness, making it easier to fall asleep and improve the overall quality of sleep. Melatonin is often regarded as a safe and effective way to enhance sleep, especially for those struggling with irregular sleep patterns.

Serotonin Increasers

Serotonin is a neurotransmitter that plays a crucial role in regulating mood, emotions, and several bodily functions, including sleep. It is primarily produced in the brain and the gastrointestinal tract, where it helps transmit signals between nerve cells. Supplementing with serotonin can have several benefits for sleep, as it is a precursor to melatonin, the hormone responsible for regulating sleep-wake cycles. Increased serotonin levels can enhance sleep quality by promoting relaxation and reducing stress, leading to a more restful and uninterrupted sleep. The most commonly prescribed antidepressants are a *selective serotonin reuptake inhibitors* (SSRIs) , SSRIs can help with moderate to severe depression. The side effects that SSRIs can cause like dizziness and drowsiness, do assist with sleep. Additionally, higher serotonin levels are associated with improved mood and a sense of well-being, which can further contribute to better sleeping patterns.

GABA

GABA, or gamma-aminobutyric acid, is a neurotransmitter that plays a crucial role in promoting relaxation and reducing anxiety, making it particularly beneficial for enhancing sleep quality. By increasing GABA levels in the brain, this supplement can help to calm the nervous system, leading to faster sleep onset and more restful sleep cycles. Users often report experiencing fewer nighttime awakenings and a feeling of overall rejuvenation upon waking. Additionally, GABA can help alleviate stress, which is a common barrier to achieving deep, restorative sleep. As a natural alternative to sleep aids, it supports a holistic approach to sleep enhancement without the risk of dependency or adverse side effects typically associated with pharmaceutical treatments.

Reshi Mushroom

Reshi mushroom, scientifically known as Ganoderma lucidum, is a renowned medicinal fungus that has been used for centuries in traditional Chinese medicine. Often referred to as the "mushroom of immortality," Reshi is celebrated for its adaptogenic properties, which help the body cope with stress. Among its numerous health benefits, Reshi is particularly noted for its positive impact on sleep functions. It is thought to promote relaxation and reduce anxiety, helping individuals achieve a more peaceful state of mind before bedtime. Additionally, Reshi mushroom may enhance overall sleep quality by regulating sleep cycles and increasing the duration of deep sleep stages. Its ability to balance hormones and support immune function further contributes to a restful night's sleep, making it a popular choice for those seeking natural remedies for sleep disturbances.

Lion's Mane

Lion's Mane mushroom, scientifically known as Hericium erinaceus, is a distinctive mushroom characterized by its long, white, shaggy spines resembling a lion's mane. This unique fungus has gained popularity in traditional medicine and wellness communities due to its potential health benefits. One of the notable positive effects of Lion's Mane mushrooms is their soothing impact on sleep. They contain compounds that may promote the production of nerve growth factor (NGF), which supports brain health and cognitive functions. Additionally, Lion's Mane has been linked to reduced anxiety and stress levels, creating a more tranquil mental state conducive to restful sleep. By improving overall nighttime relaxation, this mushroom can help enhance the quality and duration of sleep for those seeking a natural solution to sleep disturbances.

Ashwganda

Ashwagandha root, scientifically known as Withania somnifera, is a revered adaptogenic herb in traditional Ayurvedic medicine, known for its ability to help the body manage stress and promote overall well-being. This powerful herb is believed to stabilize mood by balancing cortisol levels, the hormone primarily responsible for stress, thereby reducing anxiety and enhancing feelings of calm. Additionally, Ashwagandha has been shown to improve sleep quality by promoting relaxation and reducing insomnia, leading to more restorative sleep cycles. By supporting emotional health and encouraging better sleep patterns, Ashwagandha root serves as a natural ally for those seeking to enhance their mental clarity and emotional resilience.

Kava

Kava root, derived from the kava plant (Piper methysticum), is a traditional beverage consumed in the South Pacific, particularly in countries like Fiji, Vanuatu, and Tonga. The root contains kavalactones, which are compounds known for their calming and relaxing effects. Consuming kava can promote feelings of relaxation and reduce anxiety without impairing cognitive function. It is often used as a natural remedy for stress and anxiety, aiding in social interaction by fostering a sense of well-being. Additionally, kava is believed to improve sleep quality and may have mild analgesic properties, making it a popular alternative to mainstream anxiolytics and sleep medications. However, it's essential to use kava responsibly and be aware of potential side effects and interactions with other substances.

Jatamansi

Jatamansi, a revered herb in traditional Ayurvedic (Hindu) medicine, is celebrated for its remarkable sleep benefits. It is known for its calming and soothing properties, making it an excellent natural remedy for those struggling with insomnia or restless nights. By helping to regulate the production of serotonin and melatonin, jatamansi promotes a balanced sleep cycle and eases anxiety, thus paving the way for deeper, more restorative sleep. Its ability to reduce stress and enhance relaxation allows individuals to unwind, leading to a more serene mental state and ultimately improving overall sleep quality. Incorporating jatamansi into one's nighttime routine can be a gentle yet effective way to achieve the restful slumber that many seek.

Passion Flower

Passion flower, scientifically known as Passiflora incarnata, is a flowering vine native to the southeastern United States and parts of Central and South America. This plant is notable for its unique, intricate flowers and has been used traditionally as a herbal remedy for various ailments. One of the most prominent benefits of passion flower is its potential to improve sleep quality. It contains natural compounds, such as flavonoids and alkaloids, that may help to increase levels of gamma-aminobutyric acid (GABA) in the brain, promoting relaxation and reducing anxiety. As a result, passion flower is often utilized as a natural sleep aid, helping individuals fall asleep more easily and enjoy a deeper and more restorative rest. Additionally, it may assist in alleviating symptoms of insomnia and improving overall sleep patterns.

Valerian Root

Valerian root is a herbal remedy derived from the Valeriana officinalis plant, commonly used for its calming and sedative properties. This natural supplement is often sought after for its potential to improve sleep quality and alleviate insomnia. Valerian root works by increasing the levels of a neurotransmitter called gamma-aminobutyric acid (GABA) in the brain, which helps promote relaxation and reduce anxiety. Many individuals find that taking valerian root before bedtime can help them fall asleep faster and achieve a deeper, more restorative sleep, making it a popular choice for those seeking a natural alternative to over-the-counter sleep aids.

Chamomile

Chamomile is a herb that has been used for centuries for its calming and therapeutic properties. Often consumed as a tea, chamomile is known for its ability to promote relaxation and improve sleep quality. The active compounds in chamomile, particularly apigenin, bind to specific receptors in the brain that help reduce anxiety and induce a sense of calmness. This natural sedative effect can aid in easing tension and stress, making it easier to fall asleep and stay asleep throughout the night. Additionally, chamomile possesses anti-inflammatory and antioxidant properties, which contribute to overall well-being. As a result, incorporating chamomile into a nightly routine can be an effective way to support relaxation and enhance sleep.

Vitamin D + Calcium

Taking vitamin D and calcium at night could enhance sleep quality through several mechanisms. Vitamin D plays a crucial role in regulating the sleep-wake cycle by influencing the production of melatonin, the hormone responsible for sleep onset. Adequate levels of calcium are essential for the body to efficiently utilize vitamin D, and they also contribute to the relaxation of muscles and nerves, promoting a calming effect that can facilitate falling asleep. Together, these nutrients may help to create a more restful environment for sleep by reducing nighttime awakenings and improving overall sleep architecture. Incorporating vitamin D and calcium into a nighttime routine can also signal to the body that it's time to wind down, further enhancing the quality and duration of sleep.

5-HTP

5-HTP, or 5-hydroxytryptophan, is a naturally occurring amino acid and chemical precursor to serotonin, a neurotransmitter that plays a crucial role in regulating mood and sleep. When taken as a supplement, 5-HTP is believed to enhance serotonin levels in the brain, which can improve sleep patterns by promoting a more restful and deeper sleep. Research indicates that 5-HTP may help alleviate insomnia and increase sleep quality by reducing the time it takes to fall asleep. Additionally, higher serotonin levels can contribute to an enhanced sense of well-being and relaxation (as mentioned above), further aiding in the sleep process.

Cannibis

Cannabis has gained attention for its potential benefits in improving sleep. This potential stems from its interaction with the endocannabinoid system in our bodies. The endocannabinoid system is vital for regulating various bodily functions, including sleep patterns. It helps our bodies maintain balance and adapt to changes. When it comes to sleep, this system can be particularly helpful in making adjustments that promote better rest.

The two main compounds in cannabis that contribute to its sleep-promoting effects are cannabidiol (CBD) and tetrahydrocannabinol (THC). Both of these compounds interact with the endocannabinoid system in different ways. CBD is widely recognized for its relaxing properties. It can help alleviate anxiety and stress, which are often significant barriers to falling asleep. For instance, someone dealing with a stressful day might find it hard to wind down at bedtime. Taking CBD could help calm their mind and prepare them for sleep.

On the other hand, THC is known for inducing feelings of euphoria and deep relaxation. This can be especially beneficial for those looking to unwind after a long day. For example, if someone experiences racing thoughts when they lie down at night, THC might help slow down those thoughts and bring about a more relaxed state of mind. As a result, it may become easier to drift off to sleep.

However, it is essential to note that the effectiveness of cannabis for sleep can vary significantly depending on several factors. These include the specific strain of cannabis, the dosage taken, and each individual's unique response to the compounds. Some strains may have higher levels of CBD, while others may be richer in THC. Users might need to experiment with different strains to discover which one best suits their sleep needs.

Moreover, the dosage is another important factor. Taking too little may not provide the desired benefits, while taking too much could lead to feelings of grogginess or a disrupted sleep cycle the following day. For many people, starting with a low dose and gradually increasing it until they find an optimal level is a good strategy. It is often recommended to keep a journal to track results, noting any changes in sleep patterns or feelings of restfulness.

Given these variations, it's crucial for anyone considering cannabis for sleep to approach it with a personalized mindset. What works for one person may not work for another, and understanding one's own body is key. If someone is new to using cannabis, consulting with a healthcare professional can also provide valuable guidance tailored to their particular health situation and sleep challenges. However, as I have learned, many medical practitioners will still resort to their well-known prescription medication, rather than cannabis. I am optimistic that the perception of cannabis is evolving, leading more healthcare professionals to distance themselves from the influence of large pharmaceutical companies.

*****

While these remedies bring forth intriguing possibilities, they demand a scientific context to validate centuries of anecdotal evidence. Although some studies offer promising results, it's crucial to recognize that evidence remains varied and at times inconclusive. This is not to deter use but to promote a keen awareness among those seeking these alternatives. In pursuing natural remedies, you're not just choosing tradition over science; you're integrating both to find solutions that modern medicine continues to validate and explore.

Mind-body techniques further amplify the benefits of these lifestyle changes, merging emotional well-being with physical relaxation. Practices like yoga offer gentle stretches and mindful breathing, preparing both mind and body for restful sleep. Yoga encourages mindfulness—bringing you into moment-to-moment awareness—which reduces stress and anxiety levels. Combined with aromatherapy, these practices enhance one another. Applying essential oils like lavender or sandalwood during yoga sessions infuses calming aromas into the atmosphere, deepening the relaxation experience (Vora et al., 2024). These practices can nurture a holistic balance, addressing not just physical restlessness but mental agitation that deters sleep.

It's important to keep in mind that medications and natural remedies do not deliver a one-size-fits-all solution. Each remedy can yield differing results, partly due to individual physiological differences and partly due to the remedy's inherent variability. For some, valerian root may work wonders; for others, it might offer no noticeable benefit. Success often requires a degree of experimentation, comprising a willingness to try different combinations and note personal responses. Experimentation should be approached with care, starting with lower doses and observing any changes in sleep patterns. For instance, while one might find relief in switching to a bedtime routine featuring chamomile tea, another might find greater benefit in nightly lavender aromatherapy (Vora et al., 2024).

Concrete examples can clarify these remedies' potential. Consider John, a middle-aged professional, who found that including a brief yoga routine before bed, combined with lavender oil diffusion, greatly improved his sleep quality. Meanwhile, Jane, who often wakes up in the night, saw her intermittent sleep issues lessen with the inclusion of valerian supplements in her nightly regime. Both underscore the reality that what works for one person might not for another, and *personalization is key*.

Navigating the realm of natural sleep aids demands an appreciation for both their possibilities and their limitations. Differences in individual responses underline the importance of personalized trial and error. This represents an opportunity to curate a sleep aid strategy hand-tailored to one's unique needs and biological disposition. Monitoring your sleep patterns, noting any improvements or adverse effects, will empower you to make informed decisions on which remedies or combinations offer the best support (Vora et al., 2024).

As we turn a page towards the complexities of mixing various remedies, recognizing potential interactions becomes crucial. Natural remedies, though perceived as safer, can pose risks when combined without foresight. This could lead to unintended side effects or diminish the effectiveness of each component within the mix. So, our next exploration will delve into these interactions, scrutinizing the delicate balance between potential benefits and risks involved in combining various natural sleep aids. Understanding these dynamics not only safeguards your health but enriches your journey toward achieving optimal sleep.

Risks of Mixing Remedies

Taking our previous discussion on natural remedies and prescription medication into account, it's crucial to understand the potential interactions between these and other substances. Many adults turn to herbal supplements, lifestyle changes, and mind-body techniques for sleep issues without recognizing the risks of combining them. Each remedy may have its own benefits, but mixing them indiscriminately can lead to unintended consequences. Ensuring a seamless transition from prior knowledge about natural remedies, we now consider how these potential synergies can sometimes prove harmful.

The risks of mixing various sleep aids arise from the complex chemical reactions that can occur when different substances interact. Let's look at melatonin, a common supplement used to regulate sleep cycles. When combined with alcohol, which many mistakenly believe might enhance relaxation, the potential for increased drowsiness or dizziness rises. This interaction can impair one's ability to function safely and effectively in daily activities, potentially leading to accidents or injuries if not properly managed.

Consider herbal teas made from valerian root or chamomile, recognized for their calming properties. While individually effective, combining these with over-the-counter sleep medications can amplify sedative effects to a possible dangerous levels. Without proper awareness, individuals could face challenges in waking fully or maintaining alertness the next day, impacting their professional and personal life.

Real-world examples abound, illustrating the potential pitfalls of mixing remedies. One notable case involved an individual who regularly used kava, a popular herbal remedy for anxiety, alongside prescribed sedatives. The patient experienced a significant depressive episode, necessitating hospitalization. This situation exemplifies the adverse effects that can unfold without an understanding of cross-reactions, underscoring the importance of a cautious approach to combining remedies. Personally, I do mix a prescription medication with a few natural remedies, and this has provided a good solution . However each person is different, and interactions could occur if not being careful.

To mitigate such risks, it's essential to engage healthcare professionals in discussions about sleep aid usage. By drawing on their expertise, you gain valuable insights into the interactions of various substances. When healthcare professionals are aware of all consumed supplements or medications, they can pinpoint potential risk areas and provide guidance tailored to individual health profiles and sleep needs.

Transparency in these conversations cannot be emphasized enough. Providing honest accounts of all remedies being taken allows healthcare providers to make informed recommendations. It's not simply about disclosing prescription medications; herbal supplements, vitamin intake, and lifestyle changes play significant roles in maintaining health and must be included in discussions.

The professional consultation process involves asking critical questions about the safety of combining specific remedies. Healthcare providers can recommend safe alternatives to risky combinations or adjust dosages to minimize harmful interactions. Understanding that the wisdom of trained professionals can act as a safeguard highlights the essential role they play in maintaining health when exploring remedy combinations.

Beyond professional assistance, it is advisable to adopt personal safety practices in managing sleep aids. Timing, dosage, and symptom monitoring become key procedures while navigating multiple remedies. Adherence to recommended dosages is critical, particularly since many natural supplements lack strict regulatory oversight, leading to variations in concentrations and efficacy.

Consistently monitoring symptoms provides valuable feedback on whether remedies are safe and effective. If side effects emerge, prompt consultation with a healthcare provider can prevent further complications down the line. Keeping a comprehensive log detailing remedy usage enables smooth communication with healthcare professionals, facilitating ongoing evaluation of remedy effectiveness and safety.

Emerging awareness of these risks leads naturally into a transition towards exploring the evolution of remedies. By understanding the dangers of mixing treatments, readers develop an informed appreciation for both historical and modern solutions. Acknowledging change over time reflects a journey in which past wisdom and contemporary advances converge to offer a balanced perspective on sleep management. Recognizing this intersection between past and present not only informs future choices but also honors the diverse strategies humans have employed to find restful sleep.

Thus, a structured approach to remedy usage ensures not only immediate benefits but long-term well-being, creating an informed user base that respects the power of all remedies, natural or otherwise. The next section will guide you through this evolution, comparing age-old wisdom with today's solutions, highlighting both risks and rewards. As you navigate these chapters, carry with you an understanding of the significance in every decision, informed by both history and current practice, to ensure your experiences with sleep remedies are positive, enriching, and safe.

Integration and Reflection

In previous sections, we examined how interactions between various factors can influence sleep patterns, underscoring the importance of professional consultation. Acknowledging these risks sets a crucial foundation for analyzing the benefits and applicability of both historical and modern remedies. Balancing these perspectives requires a nuanced understanding of personal needs alongside expert advice, helping to craft safe and effective sleep strategies.

Historically, many cultures have developed their own remedies to combat sleep disturbances. For instance, ancient Egyptians used natural ingredients like lettuce seeds, which they believed had sedative properties. Meanwhile, the Greeks often relied on herbal teas infused with ingredients such as chamomile and valerian root. These historical approaches reflect not only the experimental nature of societies seeking relief but also illustrate a deep trust in nature's resources.

In contrast, modern solutions often emphasize pharmaceutical intervention and technology. The development of sleep aids like melatonin supplements and CPAP machines showcases the leaps in scientific understanding and medical advancements. However, while modern methods often offer precision and proven efficacy, they can lack the holistic touch and cultural resonance found in historical practices.

Understanding how cultural factors shape these choices unpacks a rich tapestry of beliefs, traditions, and contemporary influences. Take, for example, traditional Chinese medicine (TCM), which has been practiced for thousands of years. TCM focuses on balancing the body's energies through methods like acupuncture and herbal medicine. Despite advances in science, millions worldwide still favor these techniques, blending ancient wisdom with modern lifestyle needs.

Conversely, in Western contexts, sleep solutions have historically leaned towards the scientific method, with a strong focus on identifying biological causes and treatments. This evolution has been influenced by technological innovation and behavioral studies, leading to practices such as cognitive behavioral therapy for insomnia (CBT-I discussed in Chapter 2) that combine psychology with medical insights.

The convergence and divergence of these remedies reveal how societies adapt and evolve. In cultures where traditions hold immense influence, modern approaches often incorporate elements of historical remedies to cater to cultural preferences. This interplay helps demystify how communities perceive sleep solutions, often valuing a harmonious blend of both worlds for more comprehensive results.

Consider India, where Ayurveda, an ancient healing system, provides natural sleep remedies such as ashwagandha and jatamansi. These traditional treatments are increasingly being approached through modern medical lenses, with scientific studies investigating their efficacy. The belief systems embedded in Ayurveda often resonate strongly with Indian culture, giving traditional methods an edge alongside newer, scientific developments.

On the other hand, Japanese culture, known for its technological advances, has seen a rising trend in the use of gadgets and sleep trackers. However, traditional practices such as Zen meditation and incorporating elements of nature into sleep environments still play a significant role. The Japanese concept of "inemuri" — being present while asleep — highlights how deeply ingrained cultural practices around sleep are.

Examining these examples reveals how historical and modern solutions aren't necessarily competitors but can complement one another. By acknowledging and respecting cultural influences, individuals may find a broader range of options conducive to their unique needs and lifestyles. This intersection proves fertile ground for blending age-old wisdom with cutting-edge scientific discoveries, resulting in integrated sleep solutions that respect tradition while embracing innovation.

The discussion encourages us to analyze how personal preferences, when informed by expert advice, can merge into well-rounded sleep strategies. Should someone find comfort in an herbal infusion reminiscent of their grandparents' remedies, their sleep strategy might incorporate this alongside a modern tool like a weighted blanket. By understanding the timing, dosage, and potential interactions of various remedies, people can make informed decisions that enhance safety and effectiveness.

When we look at sleep under the light of both historical and modern lenses, it becomes clear that a more comprehensive approach often involves combining insights from both. Eye masks with essential oils might echo the use of lavender in ancient Rome hellenistic society, yet today can be paired with mindfulness apps that leverage modern psychology to promote relaxation and sleepiness. This confluence of old and new, like the marriage of fact and emotion in storytelling, provides a generous coverage of options without compromise.

It is crucial to remain objective, recounting histories, cultural influences, and modern strategies without bias. This clarity helps ensure that each method's effectiveness and applicability can be objectively evaluated based on individual circumstances. When understanding the rich tapestry of historical contexts and cultural practices, it underscores the importance of inclusivity in health practices.

In sum, this exploration into the intersection of historical and modern sleep remedies invites an appreciation of diverse perspectives. By analyzing these overlapping interests, we encourage thinking beyond conventional boundaries. The ultimate goal: to foster solutions that not only improve sleep health but also honor and integrate the diverse traditions and innovations contributing to the way we approach this universal aspect of well-being.

Summary and Reflections

As we navigate the landscape of sleep remedies, from historical substances like laudanum to modern pharmaceuticals and natural alternatives, it becomes apparent that our approach to addressing sleep issues is a constantly evolving journey. Understanding these roots helps us appreciate how far we've come in balancing efficacy with safety. This knowledge guides us toward more informed choices as we embrace both the science of today and the wisdom of the past. By integrating these insights, we open new pathways for innovative and holistic solutions that prioritize safe, effective sleep health management. Moving forward, this comprehensive perspective encourages a tailored approach to sleep therapy, empowering individuals to find personalized solutions that resonate with their unique needs and cultural backgrounds.

Chapter 8

Breathing and Sleep Optimization

Have you ever noticed how some nights you go to bed, ready to fall into a deep sleep, but instead find yourself tossing and turning for hours? Breathing deeply seems almost impossible, as if something is blocking the restful slumber you seek. Maybe you've tried adjusting your pillows or switching off your phone earlier, hoping these small changes might help. But still, you wake up the next morning feeling more tired than when you went to bed. It's frustrating, isn't it? Sleep should be simple, yet for many, it's anything but.

This chapter will guide you through understanding the intricate factors that affect sleep quality, from breathing techniques and their importance, relaxing techniques to the unexpected role that sex can play in ensuring a good night's rest. By exploring these facets, we aim to equip you with practical solutions and insights to overcome your sleepless nights and achieve the peace and refreshment you deserve every time you close your eyes.

Breathing Complications and Breathing Techniques

Breathing disorders like obstructive sleep apnea (OSA) often fly under the radar despite their prevalence. These disorders cause significant disruptions in sleep cycles and result in poor sleep quality. Addressing them early is crucial in managing sleep effectively. Many people remain unaware of their condition, going undiagnosed for years. Common symptoms include chronic snoring, episodes of stopped breathing, and restless sleep marked by frequent awakenings. By paying attention to the signs and seeking medical advice, individuals can take crucial steps toward better sleep and overall health.

Breathing plays a central role in sleep quality, with OSA and other sleep-disordered breathing leading to considerable health challenges. Sleep apnea results in repeated interruptions in airflow, disturbing sleep and decreasing blood oxygen levels. One major predisposing factor is obesity, contributing to an estimated 58% of moderate to severe obstructive sleep apnea cases (Memon & Manganaro, 2021). As weight increases, so does the likelihood of these disorders, emphasizing the importance of lifestyle modifications to reduce risk.

Breath control techniques, particularly diaphragmatic breathing, offer remarkable benefits for improving sleep. This technique enhances lung capacity, relaxes the mind, and prepares the body for rest. To practice diaphragmatic breathing, start by finding a comfortable seated position. Place one hand on your chest and the other on your abdomen. This positioning helps you observe your breath and maintain focus. Inhale slowly through your nose, allowing your abdomen to expand while keeping your chest relatively still. Exhale gently through your mouth, observing the movement of your abdomen as it falls. Repeat the cycle for several minutes, focusing on slow, deep breaths. These steps may sound simple, but practice makes perfect. Over time, this technique can significantly reduce anxiety and calm the mind, facilitating deeper sleep and improving respiratory health.

Proper posture influences breathing efficiency, making it easier to practice techniques like diaphragmatic breathing. Maintaining correct posture during daily activities facilitates deeper, more effective breathing, preparing the body for better sleep at night. Think of how you slouch at work or when watching TV—remind yourself to sit upright, shoulders back, and chest open. These small adjustments support better lung function and overall relaxation.

Incorporating controlled breathing exercises into your nightly routine can build resilience against stress, allowing the mind to unwind. Anxiety often thrives on irregular breathing patterns, so focusing on even, slow breaths works as a form of meditation, driving away tension and paving the path for peaceful sleep. Regular followers of such practices report enhanced sleep quality, pointing to the profound effects on mental and physical relaxation. The calming nature of these exercises can help individuals break the cycle of restlessness and recurrent awakenings associated with conditions like OSA.

Research suggests that breathing retraining can significantly impact sleep apnea management (Courtney, 2020). Engaging in activities requiring significant breath control, like singing or playing wind instruments, can enhance muscle tone of the upper airway and improve respiratory muscle strength, both key contributors to reducing sleep-disordered breathing issues. It's not just about blowing out tunes; these activities reinforce the body's natural habit of taking in full, even breaths, combatting the inconsistency characteristic of sleep apnea.

Weight gain can significantly impact the throat due to the accumulation of excess fat around the neck area, which can lead to constriction of the airways. This narrowing can cause obstructive sleep apnea, leading to fragmented sleep and daytime fatigue. The added pressure on the throat can also contribute to increased snoring, further disrupting both the individual's sleep and that of others nearby. Additionally, the inflammation and excess tissue can make it difficult for air to flow freely, exacerbating breathing difficulties both during sleep and in daily activities. Consequently, individuals may experience compromised respiratory function, decreased vitality, and a heightened risk of other health issues related to sleep deficiency.

Breathing properly during sleep is essential; it's not just about inhaling and exhaling more deeply but doing so in a way that syncs bodily functions, resulting in authentic rest. Proper pillow support at night can help maintain spinal alignment, an often overlooked component of effective breathing. When lying in bed, use supportive pillows to keep the neck and back in a neutral position, promoting optimal air passage.

Ultimately, sleep quality is a jigsaw, and breathing is a central, often neglected piece. Addressing breathing issues through techniques like diaphragmatic breathing, posture corrections, and engagement in breath-control activities can make a measurable difference. The path to better sleep involves paying attention to these foundational aspects of breathing, integrating them into daily routines, and taking charge of one's health. As these small but significant changes become habits, individuals often find themselves sleeping more soundly and waking up refreshed.

The next section delves into how stress impacts breathing and sleep quality, broadening our understanding of the multifaceted relationship between these essential aspects of well-being.

Impact of Stress on Breathing and Sleep

In our exploration of how breathing impacts sleep quality, one cannot overlook the substantial influence of stress. Stress is notorious for exacerbating breathing issues, a direct link to compromised sleep quality. As we delve into stress and breathing, their connection becomes glaringly evident. Stress often results in shallow breathing or tachypnea, where reduced oxygen intake and increased carbon dioxide levels create a cycle of anxiety and restlessness, impacting sleep (Cronkleton, 2024). Stress triggers this type of rapid, shallow breathing, altering respiratory patterns to a degree that sleep becomes elusive.

When the body's natural relaxation processes are compromised due to inefficient breathing, the quality of sleep diminishes significantly. This connection between stress-influenced breathing and sleep is well-documented. For instance, the limbic system, responsible for emotional regulation, becomes activated during high-stress periods. As a result, high levels of anxiety disrupt the prefrontal cortex's ability to manage emotions, further disrupting sleep through erratic breathing patterns (Balban et al., 2023).

Consider the common scenario where a person's stress from daily life induces shallow breathing. This shallow breathing, often occurring without conscious awareness, leads to a physiological state unsuitable for restful sleep. The body fails to enter deeper sleep stages due to incessant activation of stress responses. This sleep disruption isn't just physical but psychological. Cognitive functions that deal with stress can also become impaired, leading to a vicious cycle of stress and sleep deprivation. The mind struggles to disengage from the day's stressors, fueling ongoing anxiety and leading to further sleep disruptions.

To break this cycle, exploring techniques that marry stress management and breathing is crucial. Breathing exercises, like diaphragmatic breathing and the 4-7-8 technique, address both components effectively.

The 4-7-8 breathing technique involves inhaling for four seconds, holding the breath for seven seconds, and exhaling for eight seconds. This practice is designed to promote relaxation and reduce stress. It is performed by inhaling deeply through the nose for four counts, holding the breath for seven counts, and then exhaling slowly through the mouth for eight counts. This cycle can be repeated four times, helping to calm the mind and body.

These practices insist on slowing down the breath, directly impacting the autonomic nervous system, thereby mitigating stress responses (Cronkleton, 2024). The effect is twofold: a calm mind and enhanced oxygen delivery systemically improve physiological conditions for sleep. Tackling stress with these practices fosters a sense of control over one's breathing and emotional state.

Another powerful method is cognitive-behavioral techniques, which guide individuals to recognize and modify stress-inducing thought patterns. Complemented by targeted breathing exercises, these can significantly alter one's response to stressors, thus revamping the mind's readiness for restful sleep. Similarly, approaching this issue holistically via yoga or tai chi manages stress by blending physical movement with regulated breathing to calm the nervous system and prepare the body for sleep.

Holistic approaches exemplify the dual role of reducing stress and enhancing sleep hygiene. Yoga, renowned for its extensive breathing focus, promotes an inward focus that eases the mind's chatter, paving the way for better night's sleep. Tai chi, with its slow, deliberate movements, fosters relaxation through synchronized breath and motion, enhancing both mental and physical calmness.

Incorporating these practices into daily life isn't overly complex. For instance, dedicating a few minutes each day to controlled breathing or a short yoga session can visibly reduce stress and boost sleep quality. Imagine beginning the day with alternate nostril breathing, a technique that balances the nervous system's functions, and ending with a simple meditative breathing practice. Over time, this forms a routine that not only enhances sleep but elevates overall well-being.

Through these perspectives, the critical role of stress management in overcoming sleep-related breathing issues becomes apparent. Reducing stress not only addresses immediate breathing disruptions but also fosters the groundwork for addressing other factors affecting sleep, such as hormonal fluctuations. As we continue our journey into understanding all facets influencing sleep, the significance of managing stress through conscious breathwork, cognitive methodologies, and lifestyle adjustments remains a primary pillar. Understanding these dynamics is foundational as we prepare to explore how other factors, including physiological changes and hormonal influences, shape our readiness for uninterrupted sleep.

Engaging with stress management isn't a solitary pursuit; it interconnects with broader well-being. Integrating these practices reinforces not just sleep but also everyday mental resilience against stress. As each breathing exercise is a step towards reclaiming breath control, it's also a leap towards embracing better sleep. With a firm comprehension of how stress management, breathing, and sleep intertwine, we lay the groundwork for further topics, ultimately steering toward an optimized state of relaxation and rest. □As we prepare to dive into how physiological responses to different activities, like sex, further intertwine with these elements, the importance of stress management and breathing as foundational to any sleep-enhancing routine stands out. Each harmonized breath, intentional movement, and mental strategy becomes an integral component of this layered approach to wellness, illustrating the broader picture of how deeply interconnected stress, breathing, and sleep truly are.

Influence of Sex on Sleep Quality

Previously, we discussed the profound impact stress management has on breathing and sleep. By addressing stress, we improve breathing patterns, laying the foundation for better sleep quality. Now, let's explore how sex similarly influences relaxation and enhances our ability to achieve restful sleep.

Sexual activity triggers the release of specific hormones that play a crucial role in relaxation and sleep induction. One key hormone, oxytocin, often dubbed the "love hormone," is released during physical intimacy. Oxytocin fosters feelings of closeness and emotional bonding, reducing stress and promoting a sense of calm. Following sexual encounters, oxytocin levels in the body increase, which can help kickstart the relaxation process necessary for falling asleep (The Relationship between Sex and Sleep, 2021).

In addition to oxytocin, endorphins are released during sexual activity, producing feelings of happiness and reducing pain perception. These "feel-good" hormones create a sense of well-being that can ease the transition into sleep. The combination of oxytocin and endorphins contributes to a state of relaxation, fostering a conducive environment for slumber (How Sex Affects Sleep, 2022).

To illustrate these effects, consider a couple who engages in an intimate encounter before bedtime. Both partners experience a surge in oxytocin and endorphins, which can help soothe anxieties from the day. The calming atmosphere and intimate connection pave the way for a more tranquil entry into sleep. These neurochemical changes underline the significance of sexual activity in promoting healthier sleep habits.

Beyond hormonal changes, the physical exertion involved in sexual activity often leads to fatigue. The energy expended during sex can contribute to a state of relaxation, facilitating deeper and more restorative sleep. The act itself becomes an extension of the day's physical activity, culminating in tiredness that encourages restfulness (How Sex Affects Sleep, 2022).

Let's pivot to examining the timing of sexual activity in relation to sleep. Engaging in intimacy shortly before bedtime can significantly enhance relaxation and readiness for sleep. This timing allows the body to drift into the rhythm of slowing down, mirroring the natural wind-down process that precedes slumber (The Relationship between Sex and Sleep, 2021).

However, it's important to consider individual preferences and experiment with what timing practice works best. For instance, while some may find nighttime intimacy ideal for sleep induction, others may experience overstimulation that hinders their ability to fall asleep immediately. The key is to tailor timing to personal needs, ensuring that sexual activity aligns with individual sleep goals.

Let's delve into the intricate relationship between sexual health and sleep disorders. Addressing sexual health can indirectly improve sleep by alleviating certain disturbances. For example, resolving issues of sexual dysfunction can enhance relationship satisfaction, leading to reduced stress and anxiety, which improves sleep quality (How Sex Affects Sleep, 2022).

Moreover, the therapeutic benefits of incorporating intimacy into relationships extend beyond the physical realm. Emotional intimacy and a healthy sex life play pivotal roles in mental health improvements and enhanced sleep quality. Emotional connections foster an environment of trust and security, which is essential for restful sleep (The Relationship between Sex and Sleep, 2021).

Consider an individual struggling with anxiety that disrupts their sleep. By focusing on nurturing emotional intimacy, they create a supportive environment conducive to relaxation. The emotional reassurance gained through intimate connections can significantly ease mental burdens, making it easier to achieve restful sleep. This demonstrates the positive influence emotional connections have on overall sleep comfort and satisfaction.

As we transition to the upcoming discussion on sleep positions and posture, it's vital to understand the interplay between intimacy and physical comfort. The position we choose for intimacy often influences our sleep posture, impacting comfort and restfulness. You'll soon discover how different sleep positions affect your comfort, health, and the importance of adjusting sleep environments to support proper posture for improved sleep.

Understanding how sex influences sleep requires a holistic view of physiological mechanisms, timing experimentation, and emotional connections. This comprehensive approach allows us to harness the benefits of intimacy for superior sleep quality. Exploring these nuances reveals the intricate connections between intimacy and slumber, providing valuable insights into achieving restorative and rejuvenating sleep.

Influence of Seasonal Allergies

Seasonal allergies, particularly in the spring, can significantly impact respiratory function, leading to various breathing issues. When pollen levels rise during this season, many individuals experience heightened allergic reactions characterized by symptoms such as nasal congestion, sneezing, and throat irritation. These symptoms can obstruct airflow, making it difficult to breathe comfortably, especially at night. As nighttime nasal congestion worsens, individuals may struggle to find a suitable position to sleep or breathe through their mouths, leading to disturbed sleep patterns and potential sleep deprivation. To help manage seasonal allergies, there are several approaches individuals can consider. First, monitoring pollen counts can help someone know when to limit their time outdoors. Various weather apps and websites provide this information, allowing allergic individuals to plan their outdoor activities accordingly. For example, staying inside on high pollen days can minimize exposure to allergens, which is important for maintaining respiratory comfort.

Another practical step is to create an allergy-friendly home environment. Keeping windows closed during high pollen days can prevent allergens from entering the home while also using air purifiers with HEPA filters to capture pollen and other allergens. Cleaning frequently can help reduce the dust and other particles that may aggravate symptoms. Simple actions like regularly washing bedding and vacuuming with a high-efficiency vacuum cleaner can make a significant difference in indoor air quality.

Over-the-counter medications can also be very effective in managing allergy symptoms. Antihistamines can relieve itching, sneezing, and runny noses, while decongestants can help clear nasal passages. For those with more severe symptoms, it is advisable to consult a healthcare professional who may recommend stronger prescription medications or allergy shots to provide long-term relief. Knowing what options are available is essential for individuals who wish to navigate allergy season with greater ease.

In addition to medical treatments, certain lifestyle adjustments can also help alleviate allergy symptoms. Staying hydrated is important, as it can keep mucus thin and help with breathing. Eating a balanced diet rich in vitamins can support the immune system, making it better equipped to handle allergens. Some individuals may also find relief through alternative therapies like acupuncture or herbal remedies, but these should be approached with caution and ideally discussed with a healthcare provider.

Life during the spring months can be challenging, as the interplay of insufficient sleep and persistent breathing issues often leads to heightened exhaustion, impaired focus, and a diminished quality of life. We may not think of this as a contributing factor, but these hidden influences need to be taken into consideration when attempting to have a good night's sleep.

Posture's Role in Sleep Health

Understanding how our sleep posture influences our well-being resonates with the knowledge shared earlier on the physiological and emotional effects of sex on sleep. Just as timing and emotional connections can refine sleep quality, recognizing our sleep posture's role can augment restfulness and health. Shifting into a new focus on sleep posture, we delve into how various positions—on one's side, back, or stomach—each carry unique effects on health and comfort. Perhaps you've noticed, if you're struggling with back pain, sleeping on your back might not be your initial thought for relief. However, research marks this position for keeping your spine neutral, reducing you're a potential for discomfort. Placing a pillow under your knees can further enhance spine alignment unless pregnancy steers you clear, citing circulation concerns (The Best — and Worst — Sleep Positions for Back Pain, 2024).

On the other hand, sleeping on your side emerges as a popular alternative, second only to back sleeping for spinal health. It can mitigate back pain and support those with sleep apnea or snoring, as open airways foster smoother breathing (The Best — and Worst — Sleep Positions for Back Pain, 2024). Straightening your legs and tucking a pillow between your knees promotes symmetry, reducing strain on your spine. However, curling into the fetal position, while common and comforting, often leads to alignment issues, potentially causing aches due to uneven weight distribution. New habits like untucking your chin and relaxing your knees can ease tension in this position.

Stomach sleeping, meanwhile, attracts much criticism. As spine experts like Dr. Raymond J. Hah note, it flattens your spine's natural curve, contributing to muscle and joint pressure and forcing uncomfortable neck rotations (The Best — and Worst — Sleep Positions for Back Pain, 2024). Although changing positions can feel like a daunting shift, the consistent relationship between pain and sleep quality encourages reevaluating habitual practices. As we examine these positions, it's essential to recognize how environment complements posture in comfort. Elements like mattress firmness, pillow shape, and bedding influence posture, playing a crucial role in overall sleep quality. A firm mattress supports spinal neutrality, while the right pillow height aligns the head with the spine, preventing neck strains.

Yet, posture's beauty lies in individual comfort. Our unique anatomy and preferences should always guide us. Environmental tweaks—like modifying mattress firmness—are strategies to tailor comfort. Integrating such changes inspires healthier spinal habits, reducing the risk of back pain and fostering uninterrupted sleep. Moving to a compelling study by Levendowski et al. (2019), we uncover the intricate links between sleep position and neurodegenerative diseases. Findings show longer durations in supine sleep correlate with neurodegenerative disorders like Alzheimer's and Parkinson's. These insights spark curiosity about how gravity influences brain blood flow, impacting protein clearance. As these proteins, such as tau and Aβ, accumulate in the brain, understanding their movement's ease during various sleep positions becomes more vital (Levendowski et al., 2019).

This connection encourages us to consider sleep position monitoring as part of broader health strategies, especially in aging populations where clearance processes change with naturally shallower breaths and decreased arterial pulsatility (Levendowski et al., 2019). Adjusting routines, like avoiding prolonged supine sleep, might enhance these processes. Such information reinforces the significance of tailored posture techniques, especially for those noticing cognitive shifts or facing increased neurodegenerative risks. A future with more focused studies might refine our understanding even further, shedding light on how changing sleep positions affects cognitive health.

Wrapping up the discussion on posture's pivotal role in sleep quality, we linger on how varied positions influence both immediate and long-term health. Whether targeting back pain, refining neurocognitive outcomes, or maximizing daily rejuvenation through more restful sleep, paying attention to posture's specifics presents a powerful ally in your sleep-enhancing toolkit. Aligning our discussions, these considerations remind us that sleep resembles a complex puzzle—one where physical posture is just a piece. Shifting focus to evening habits, including how we consume media before bed, promises to enrich our broader conversation about optimizing sleep.

As we prepare to explore how pre-bed routines, such as choosing between reading or watching television, contribute to sleep quality, it's essential to approach the topic as part of an interconnected whole. Our daily habits and routines serve as extensions of our understandings from posture, merging into an overall picture aimed at enhancing sleep health. Through examining these, we anticipate offering a fuller insight into how various lifestyle choices can shape the nature and quality of our rest, reinforcing the vital role sleep plays in maintaining our overall well-being and lifestyle satisfaction.

Media Consumption's Impact on Sleep

In our earlier exploration of posture and sleep positions, we acknowledged that the physical body needs comfort and support to properly relax. Now, as we shift focus to mental relaxation facilitated through media consumption, it's equally vital to assess how different types of evening activities affect our ability to unwind and prepare for sleep. The consumption of media, including television and reading, represents diverse pathways to cognitive engagement, each with distinct impacts on the sleep cycle.

Evening television watching poses unique challenges in terms of its impact on sleep cycles compared to reading. We know that screens from devices emit blue light, which research has shown can influence the natural sleep-wake cycle. As we discussed, this blue light can suppress melatonin production, the hormone responsible for sleep induction, thereby delaying sleep onset (Hale, 2018; Alshoaibi et al., 2023). As a result, the evening screen time spent in front of a TV is more likely to result in stunted sleep initiation and disrupted cycles, leading to poor sleep quality. The content's fast-paced and stimulating nature could further exacerbate these disruptions by keeping the brain alert, contrary to the natural wind-down process our bodies need. (More on this in the next chapter focusing on Technology.)

In contrast, reading a physical book offers an alternative pathway towards relaxation, lacking the disruptive blue light and requiring a type of slow engagement that can enhance cognitive rest. When reading, especially material with calming narratives or informative content, the brain enters a subdued state, actively sifting through stories or concepts at a soothing pace. This process can help reduce mental clutter by guiding attention away from the day's stresses and lowering arousal levels, effectively preparing the body for sleep.

Consider a scenario where someone decides to catch up on a suspenseful TV series (or watch the news) before bed. This choice, though entertaining or informative, might lead to overstimulation. The excitement and fast narrative shifts command intense cognitive engagement and elevate heart rates, mirroring the effect observed in studies on video games and violent media (Hale, 2018). In such cases, instead of aiding relaxation, television serves as a stimulant, hindering the transition into sleep. When the content on TV is thrilling or when episodes end on cliffhangers, viewers might experience restlessness and a heightened urge to continue watching, further delaying sleep.

On the flip side, picking up a novel or a favorite non-fiction piece can do wonders in steering the mind away from the daily grind. As one reads, the imagination becomes engaged in a linear and often meditative manner. Anytime readers encounter soothing content or narratives with familiar outcomes, the mind is eased into a state of tranquility. This mental quietude is beneficial, allowing sleep-promoting hormones like melatonin to follow their natural course without interference from artificial light, creating a smoother passage to rest.

Interestingly, even here, content choice plays a critical role. For instance, reading material that's distressing or overly challenging can act against this calming intention. Therefore, much like with television, one must be discerning about the content type. Light, easy-to-digest stories or educational reads are the allies of a good night's sleep, as they engage the mind without inciting undue excitement or anxiety.

Emphasizing personal preferences shapes a nighttime routine that seamlessly integrates into the individual's life. Perhaps one finds nonfiction or gentle narratives excellent cognitive soothers and leans towards such choices regularly. Over time, these consistent habits can condition the mind into viewing the reading hour as a precursor to rest, strengthening the association between certain content types and sleep onset.

Moreover, the key to establishing these pre-sleep routines lies in the awareness of time spent on devices. Individuals often underestimate how long they linger before screens, oblivious to the creeping sleep disturbances that follow their screen-intensive evenings (Alshoaibi et al., 2023). Incorporating structured limits on screen time and consciously opting for a reading session can make a significant difference in the sleep experience. Setting alarms to remind oneself to begin bedtime prep with a book, rather than automatically pressing "next episode," is a proactive stance that aligns with healthier media consumption habits.

As these media habits become entrenched, individuals are more likely to notice improvements in both sleep quality and daytime alertness. The awareness that television could stimulate rather than relax encourages even enthusiasts to seek balance and moderation. By recognizing that screen time's impacts are not identical across all media forms or content types, individuals can tailor their evening activities towards those proven to foster healthier sleep environments.

Ultimately, understanding the nuances of how media consumption affects sleep helps in crafting balanced evening routines. Through awareness and choice, individuals can pursue harmonious pre-sleep activities that align more closely with relaxation goals. Balancing time between passive screen-based media and active reading stems from insightful observation and consideration, promoting a continuity of mental and physical restfulness. Sleep cycles benefit as a consequence, with quality and duration improving through meaningful engagement with media that respects the body's innate rhythms.

Final Insights

As we draw this chapter to a close, it's clear that a variety of factors intricately affect our sleep quality. From mastering breathing techniques and understanding the influence of stress, seasonal factors, and intimacy, to considering posture habits and mindful media consumption, each element plays a critical role. Now that we understand these influences, we can empower ourselves with practical strategies to enhance our rest. Focusing on breathing techniques like diaphragmatic breathing, managing stress, engaging in healthy intimacy, and adopting supportive sleep postures are essential steps toward better sleep. Similarly, choosing calming pre-sleep activities over stimulating ones helps align our bodies and minds for rest. By integrating these insights into daily routines, individuals can pave the way for restful nights and energetic days, transforming sleep from elusive to achievable.

Chapter 9

Technology's Intrusion into Sleep

That damn clock. Sitting next to our bed mocking us. You watching it; it watching you. 2:17 a.m. Despite our exhaustion, sleep remains elusive, slipping through our fingers like sand. Just a few hours ago, we had been scrolling through our phone in bed, losing track of time while browsing social media and responding to messages. Our intentions were innocent enough—catch up with friends and relax after a long day—but now the weight of regret settled heavily on our chest.

This story is far from unique; it's a plight shared by many adults who find their nights disrupted by the temptation of technology. Those late-night screen sessions, glowing blue against the darkness, not only delay sleep onset but also affect the quality of rest. As we explore this chapter, we'll delve into the intricate ways technology intrudes upon our sleep routines and discuss actionable steps for reclaiming our nights from digital distractions.

The Role of Computers and Blue Light on our Sleep

In our increasingly digital world, the impact of screen time on sleep quality is a growing concern. Many devices, from smartphones to laptops, emit blue light, a particular type of light that can significantly disrupt our sleep cycles. Blue light exposure is known to suppress the production of melatonin, a hormone vital for maintaining our circadian rhythms and ensuring restful sleep (Silvani et al., 2022). Understanding the physiological effects of blue light can motivate us to adopt better technology-related habits to improve sleep quality.

The hormone melatonin plays a crucial role in signaling the body to prepare for sleep. Under natural conditions, melatonin levels rise in the evening, inducing drowsiness and facilitating the transition to sleep. However, blue light, primarily emitted by electronic screens, can interrupt this process by reducing melatonin production, thus delaying sleep onset and affecting overall sleep quality (Alshoaibi et al., 2023). This makes it harder for individuals to fall asleep quickly and maintain a restful state throughout the night.

Awareness of our natural sleep cycles and technology's influence on these cycles empowers us to make healthier choices. For instance, using blue light filters on devices can significantly alleviate blue light exposure in the evening, enabling melatonin production to proceed uninterrupted. Simple adjustments like this not only improve sleep quality but also enhance your daytime alertness and performance. Additionally, experts recommend reducing screen usage by limiting device interaction at least an hour before bedtime. This practice can help re-establish natural circadian rhythms, allowing for a more restful sleep (Silvani et al., 2022).

Despite the convenience and entertainment value they offer, digital devices can disrupt sleep patterns if used excessively. Nearly two-thirds of teenagers often fail to achieve the recommended duration of sleep, largely due to increased screen time before bed (Alshoaibi et al., 2023). Prioritizing tech-free time before sleep becomes essential for breaking the cycle of sleeplessness associated with frequent device use. One of the strategies involves creating a calming bedtime routine that doesn't involve screens. This might mean engaging in relaxing activities such as reading a physical book, practicing meditation, or taking a warm bath, all of which can help prepare the mind and body for sleep.

Educating ourselves and others about the importance of good sleep hygiene, especially in the context of technology use, can lead to significant improvements in overall health. It's important to encourage discussions around sleep habits and explore actionable steps to limit device usage at night. For instance, setting a fixed schedule for winding down each evening can help train the body to recognize when it's time to shift towards sleep. Also, adjusting the environment to support better sleep, such as dimming lights and using blackout curtains, can complement efforts to reduce screen exposure.

Creating mindfulness around daily technology habits allows individuals to develop a more balanced relationship with their devices, thereby minimizing their negative impacts on sleep. Taking conscious steps towards adjusting screen time habits can ultimately result in healthier sleep patterns and increased energy levels during the day. Additionally, involving family members or roommates in these efforts can foster a supportive environment, making it easier to adhere to healthier habits (Silvani et al., 2022).

When implemented consistently, these mindful habits contribute to a significant reduction in insomnia cycles linked to excessive blue light exposure. As sleep improves, you may notice enhancements in mood and cognitive function, aiding in better decision-making and stress management during waking hours. Such benefits extend beyond individual well-being, positively impacting social interactions and work performance.

As we continue to explore ways to improve sleep hygiene, the upcoming section will delve into another critical aspect — work-related stressors that often interfere with the ability to unwind before sleep. Understanding how stress affects sleep provides further insights into comprehensive strategies for promoting restful nights. By addressing both technological and occupational influences, you can formulate a holistic approach to optimizing your sleep environment and routines, ultimately fostering a more restorative sleep experience.

Transitioning to address workplace stress emphasizes the interconnectedness of different factors affecting sleep. This approach ensures a holistic understanding of how daily routines, including technology usage and workplace dynamics, interact to impact sleep quality. By integrating these insights, you can tailor strategies to reduce the interference of both screens and stressors on your sleep, leading to enhanced relaxation and overall health.

The Role of Afterhours Work on our Sleep

Smartphones and tablets stationed by our beds appear innocuous but can morph into unwelcome sleep disruptors. Those evil late-night vibrations from text messages or email notifications can jolt you awake just as you're about to drift off, derailing precious sleep cycles. Some people keep these devices within arm's reach, justifying it as a necessity. But are they? The habitual check for late-night company messages easily extends into a quick social media scroll or a news update, setting off another hour of screen time. By assessing whether constant accessibility benefits your sleep, you could discover that these devices do more harm than help. As enticing as it may be to have everything just a swipe away, creating a buffer between sleep time and these gadgets could spare you unnecessary sleep interruptions.

Sleep apps present another paradox of bedside technology. On the one hand, they offer valuable data and insights into sleep patterns, providing users with charts and graphs that illustrate sleep stages, duration, and quality. For some, seeing this information can enhance their understanding of their sleep habits and inspire efforts to improve them. On the other hand, striving to hit ideal sleep goals may spark unintended stress. Anxiety can creep in when the app displays subpar sleep scores, prompting worry about not getting enough rest. For example, a user might wake up feeling refreshed but quickly doubts that feeling upon seeing the app rate their sleep poorly. This dynamic shows how valuable tools can become stressors, shifting the focus from restful relaxation to performance pressure.

The idea of crafting personalized bedtime routines using technology pivots on transforming this narrative from stimulation to relaxation. Imagine setting up a calm wind-down playlist with your favorite soothing tunes or exploring guided meditations that offer a gentle path to sleep. By customizing these options, technology becomes a tool for easing into rest rather than an obstacle. Perhaps you'd enjoy the sound of ocean waves or a gentle voice guiding you through deep breathing exercises. These intentional uses of technology can promote relaxation and help ease the transition from wakefulness to slumber. By shifting how devices are used before bed, you create an opportunity for positive incorporation rather than exclusion.

Shaping tech-free zones starts by establishing clear boundaries regarding device use. Consider leaving smartphones charging in the living room or silencing notifications for apps while you sleep. This change can greatly impact sleep quality (Setting Healthy Boundaries at Work - Workplace Strategies for Mental Health, 2023). Removing devices from the bedroom nurtures spaces where deep rest and recovery flourish, unimpeded by alerts or the temptation to engage with a glowing screen. Crafting this tranquil environment may feel different initially, but simple rules could gradually become second nature. Those intentional boundaries could help you associate the bedroom with peaceful rest, not mental stimulation.

Encouraging reflection helps spotlight room for improvement in your routine. You might introspectively question your current habits and their alignment with optimal sleep quality. Inviting you to reassess these behaviors over time offers new opportunities to refine them, advancing health priorities to support sleep. Prioritizing environments conducive to a good night's rest should become a central life value, stepping beyond the realm of wishful thinking. Certainly, these careful assessments of technological use at night might not change sleepers' habits overnight—but there's freedom in embracing awareness as a transformative tool.

When it comes to bedside technology, there's an opportunity to embrace thoughtful adjustments that don't demand shunning gadgets altogether. Rather, exploring mindful use can foster better habits and relationships with technology. By understanding the balance between benefits and drawbacks, you can wield tech to enhance well-being instead of sabotaging it. This fine-tuning shifts nighttime routines from sporadic interruptions to cohesive, calming rituals. Instead of staring into scenes of vibrant blue light when your head hits the pillow, cultivate spaces that invite unwinding. Empowered by these approaches, you may discover pockets of rest that build a stronger foundation for dealing with daily challenges. Sleep positions itself as a silent but key player in juggling the demands of modern life. While the allure of staying constantly connected to our digital world tempts us, it's crucial to carefully shape these interactions, especially in spaces designed for rest. By consciously prioritizing sleep quality, you safeguard your mental and physical resources, ultimately enriching your life.

If anything, it's key to remember that tech doesn't have to be the enemy of sleep. Reimagining its application can lead to a friendship where technology incentivizes relaxation and bolsters quality of life. Building tech-free zones allows us to remember the timeless wisdom of simple, techless rest. Doing so will ensure a better balance, fostering spaces of true respite. We don't have to leave technology behind to achieve rest and recovery. Rather, through tailored routines and introspection, we're capable of fostering environments that nurture rest, while still keeping pace with technological advancement. Here's to the mindful crafting of our nightly retreats gathering the benefits while pausing sleep's disruptions. A concerted effort towards balance could open avenues to reclaiming the night's promise of restorative slumber. Recognizing technology's role presents an exciting opportunity for renewed habits that not only encourage better sleep but ultimately impact the broader tapestry of our daily experiences.

Bedside Use of Technology & Sleep Apps

The previous discussion on work-related stressors highlighted how these stress elements can impact our ability to unwind and relax before bedtime. Just like stress from work, the presence of technology—especially devices within arm's reach of our beds—can create further disruptions to our sleep quality. Smartphones, tablets, and other gadgets are no longer just tools for productivity; they have infiltrated the personal space of our bedrooms, often destabilizing our restful environments.

The allure of having technology nearby often stems from a desire for convenience, whether it's checking the weather, sending a quick message, or scrolling through social media before sleep. However, these devices can be the source of numerous disturbances. Alerts and notifications, with their blinking lights or buzzing vibrations, constantly compete for our attention, pulling us away from a restful state. This triggers frequent awakenings that fragment sleep, disrupting sleep cycles that are essential for achieving deep, restorative sleep.

In the modern age, our connection to these devices can feel compulsive. The impulse to check a smartphone one last time before drifting off to sleep is not uncommon. Yet, this habit poses significant challenges to sleep continuity. Each glance at the screen exposes us to the glow of short-wavelength, or "blue" light, known to interfere with melatonin secretion. Research indicates that reading on a smartphone without a blue-light filter elevates cortisol levels in the morning while decreasing morning alertness (Höhn et al., 2021). This aligns with the reports of decreased subjective sleepiness during smartphone use at night (Höhn et al., 2024).

One might argue the merits of sleep apps designed to track and analyze sleep patterns, offering insights into our nocturnal habits. While these apps promise enhanced understanding, they can also induce anxiety about meeting particular sleep metrics. Similar to how keeping score of calories can impact our eating habits, obsessing over sleep numbers might make us more anxious, thereby negatively impacting the actual quality of sleep. This focus on metrics can turn the sleep experience into a numbers game, overshadowing the natural circadian rhythm and the body's innate cues for rest.

Beside personal gadgets, other bedroom technology like televisions can also contribute to sleep disruption. Watching late-night shows or indulging in binge-watching series can delay sleep onset, as the dramatic narratives and bright screens stimulate cognitive and emotional responses that are not conducive to winding down.

It's important for us, as individuals, to critically assess the necessity of these nighttime technological companions. The decision to have these devices within easy reach should be examined, just like we scrutinize other lifestyle choices for their long-term impacts. The relevance of bedside technology should be considered in terms of its potential to benefit versus its potential to intrude into restful sleep. Evaluating the indispensability of gadgets can help prioritize better sleep hygiene over the convenience of connectivity.

To mitigate these impacts, attention should be drawn to mindful technology use. This involves creating longer periods of disconnection from devices before bedtime, adjusting screen settings to filter out blue light, and employing technology-free zones within the bedroom. These actions enable the body to transition into a sleep-ready mode more efficiently.

In addition, small habit changes, like placing the smartphone across the room to reduce the urge for late-night impulse checks, can be highly effective. The absence of easily reachable technology makes way for other pre-sleep routines that encourage relaxation, such as reading printed books or listening to soothing music.

As we consider the role of gadgets in our bedtime rituals, envision the bedroom as a sanctuary for rest. Darkness tells the body that it's time to sleep, while silence quiets the mind from the chaos of daily life. By preserving this sanctuary from persistent digital interruptions, we honor the body's natural need for rest.

Moving forward, you will the opportunity to explore practical ways to integrate these changes. The following sections delve into strategies like using night mode settings, managing alert preferences, and establishing device-free intervals. These tactics can nudge us towards more harmonious sleep practices, ultimately supporting better physical and mental health.

By embracing conscious disengagement from technology at night, we not only enhance our individual sleep environments but also improve our day-to-day productivity and well-being. With proper adjustments, the role of technology in our lives doesn't have to be contradictory to restful sleep. Rather, by understanding its effects, we can set better boundaries that respect our body's innate rhythms and maximize our overall quality of life.

Techniques for Reducing Tech Impact

Managing technology's influence over sleep starts by adjusting our device settings, particularly utilizing night mode to reduce blue light exposure. This seemingly simple maneuver significantly impacts sleep quality. The process begins in your device's settings menu, where you select display options. From here, activating the night mode is straightforward—set it to automatically engage during evening hours. This proactive adjustment supports both immediate and prolonged sleep benefits by reducing the intensity of light exposure, allowing our bodies to unwind and prepare for rest. By managing this exposure, night mode helps bridge technology use and healthy sleep.

To further balance technology's role in your evening routine, establish a digital curfew—a scheduled time each night when devices are set aside. Begin by choosing a time at least an hour before bedtime, communicated clearly with family or roommates. Gradually reduce device usage leading up to this curfew. In real-world scenarios, implementing this routine results in improved mental clarity and relaxation. For instance, individuals who adopted this practice reported experiencing less cognitive noise at night, leading to a smoother transition into sleep. Olson and colleagues have shown that reduced screen time correlates with better sleep quality in adolescents, illustrating potential benefits in adults as well (Olson et al., 2014).

Introducing mindfulness practices offers an engaging alternative to screen time, nurturing a tranquil pre-sleep environment. Consider reading physical books over digital ones, allowing the sensory experience of handling a book to replace screen-mediated experiences. Locate a cozy reading spot, select a genre that captivates you, and set a timer to moderate your sessions. For those less inclined to read, practicing deep breathing exercises serves as another excellent method. Choose a quiet space to sit or lie down, close your eyes, and focus on your breath. Gradually inhale through your nose, hold, and exhale through your mouth. These activities calm the mind and body, offering a naturally conducive pre-sleep ritual that facilitates a peaceful transition to rest.

Routine assessment of technology use can enhance self-awareness and ensure balanced habits. Make it a weekly task to track your screen time diligently. This activity aids in highlighting peak usage periods, offering insight into their direct impact on sleep quality. Recording this information helps identify patterns and triggers, encouraging conscious adaptations that prioritize restorative sleep. For example, one participant noticed their highest screen time coincided with diminished sleep, leading them to adjust their evening habits. Such deliberate modifications can incrementally better sleep, emphasizing mindfulness in monitoring digital consumption.

Let's examine some actionable steps that foster this balance extensively. When attempting to mitigate technology's adverse effects on sleep, total elimination often seems daunting. Instead, focus on gradual modifications that align with personal circumstances. This approach is vital for promoting adherence and facilitating lasting change. Engage friends or family by sharing these adjustments, creating an environment of accountability and mutual support and collectively enjoying improved rest.

Emphasize the necessity of tech-free zones, particularly within the bedroom. Removing electronic devices from sleeping areas minimizes temptation and distractive potential, promoting a sleep-centric atmosphere. Some households find success designating specific spaces, like family rooms or kitchens, for charging devices overnight. Such spaces inherently guard against habitual nighttime tech use, protecting vital sleep hours.

The effectiveness of these strategies lies in their simplicity. Incorporating them into daily life enriches mental and physical well-being while safeguarding against technology's disruptive nocturnal effects. Evidence suggests a close relationship between consistent downtime and improved sleep quality. Studies find enforced tech-free time facilitates not only relaxation but also fosters environments ripe for human connection (Fuller et al., 2017).

Continual adaptation and reevaluation remain critical. Technology endlessly evolves, continuously challenging our sleep habits. Staying informed with media and scientific updates positively influences personal strategies. Consider subscribing to newsletters offering insights or joining forums where community members share effective practices. This engagement fosters a proactive approach, preventing stagnation in restorative habits.

Efforts to manage bedtime technology usage shine in their regular application, not temporary challenge. Consistency nurtures meaningful results, embedding healthy sleep foundations that rely on steadiness and dedication. Encouraging these habits extends beyond individual gains, as they profoundly shape collective household practices. Families establishing norms around digital consumption witness improved overall rest, recognizing technology's role but thoughtfully curtailing its disruptions.

The contributors to sleep improvement come not from a single solution but from a comprehensive **compilation** of time-tested techniques, each adjusting uniquely to personal needs and dynamics. Embrace creativity, encouraging flexibility in trial variations. Whether it involves alternating reading genres, exploring new mindfulness techniques, or reassessing digital curfews, these bespoke undertakings craft individualized change that perseveres. In implementing these strategies, individuals take the pivotal helm of managing their nighttime environments, guiding themselves toward healthier, more restorative sleep.

In seeking these changes, remember their execution need not be isolated. Many global communities unite under the common goal of understanding and mitigating technology's bedtime encroachment. Joining like-minded individuals or groups nurtures accountability and collective learning, facilitating ever-evolving resources that enrich counteractive strategies. As you explore these methods and opportunities, recognize that the balance you craft empowers a lifetime of refreshed, invigorated mornings bolstered by healthy, technology-conscious nights.

Concluding Thoughts

Having delved into the impact of technology on our sleep routines, it is evident that being mindful about device usage can significantly enhance sleep quality. By understanding how blue light affects our melatonin production and circadian rhythms, we can make informed decisions to improve our health. Simple actions like reducing screen time before bed, using blue light filters, and establishing tech-free zones can lead to better sleep patterns and increased daytime alertness. Moving forward, prioritizing these adjustments allows us to reclaim restful nights and harness the transformative power of sleep. With renewed awareness and conscious efforts, we can reshape our nightly habits, ultimately enriching both our individual well-being and our ability to navigate daily challenges.

Chapter 10

Meditation for Sleep Improvement

Late into the night, Nicki found herself staring at the ceiling, her mind refusing to quiet down. The events of the day replayed over and over, each thought seemingly louder than the last as she tried desperately to find some rest. She had read countless articles promising quick fixes and watched an endless stream of videos on YouTube, all suggesting ways to get better sleep. Yet, here she was again, struggling with exhaustion that seemed to be permanently etched into her bones.

Sound sleep seemed like a distant dream for Emma, as it does for many adults who find themselves trapped in an unending cycle of restless nights and tired days. This chapter delves into meditation practices, exploring how they can offer not just relief but a path to restful nights by gently guiding you away from daily stressors towards a peaceful slumber.

Incorporating Meditation Practices for Sleep Improvement

Aside from a warm bath before bed, there are mindful ways to relax the body. Meditation serves as a valuable tool for improving sleep by promoting relaxation and reducing stress. When we meditate, we engage in practices that help quiet the mind, allowing the body to prepare for sleep. Incorporating meditation into your nightly routine can create a peaceful buffer between the day's chaos and the restful night you desire. The calmness fostered by meditation can counter the racing thoughts and tension that often make falling asleep a challenge (Nunez, 2020).

Mindfulness Meditation stands out as an effective method, focusing on the present moment while non-judgmentally acknowledging and letting go of wandering thoughts. This practice cultivates an awareness of your consciousness, breath, and body. Begin by finding a quiet space to sit or lie down in a comfortable position. Close your eyes and take slow, deep breaths, inhaling for ten counts and exhaling for ten. As thoughts surface, notice them without judgment and gently return your attention to your breathing (Nunez, 2020). Over time, these mindful moments can reduce anxiety, providing mental reprieve from stressors and setting the stage for improved sleep quality (Nunez, 2020).

Guided Visualization offers another avenue for relaxation. With this technique, you visualize calming scenes, such as a tranquil beach or a serene meadow, to steer your mind away from daily worries. Imagine the warmth of the sun on your skin or the gentle rustle of leaves, which can help transport you to a place of peace. These visualizations serve as a powerful distraction, helping you ease into sleep effortlessly. Tailor these mental images to suit your preferences, ensuring they resonate personally to maximize relaxation (Nunez, 2020). Personally, I used to meditate often, but with increasing work schedules and life demands, I find little time. Therefore, if I am having difficulty sleeping, I use the visualization method. However I alter the process – instead of visualizing a calm scene, I visualize a black piece of paper. I concentrate on the "nothingness" of this black paper. It often helps in calming my mind and "unfocus" my overactive mind.

Breathwork, such as the 4-7-8 method (discussed in Chapter 8), is a simple yet effective technique for stabilizing the mind. The rhythm of controlled breathing acts as a natural sedative, helping your nervous system enter a state conducive to sleep. Incorporating breathwork into your nightly ritual can quickly become a soothing aspect of your bedtime routine, especially on nights when stress threatens to derail your rest (Nunez, 2020).

Acupuncture is an ancient therapeutic practice that effectively promotes muscle relaxation and alleviates tension throughout the body. (Although it is not a kind of meditation, it is a way to physically relax the body.) By stimulating specific acupressure points, acupuncture encourages the release of endorphins and improves blood circulation, which helps to soothe tight muscles and reduce pain. This calming effect extends beyond physical relaxation, as acupuncture can also alleviate stress and anxiety, common contributors to insomnia. By restoring balance within the body and calming the nervous system, acupuncture assists individuals in achieving a deeper, more restful sleep, making it a valuable tool for those struggling with sleep disturbances.

Another meditation practice that can significantly enhance relaxation is the **Body Scan**. It involves gradually focusing attention on different parts of the body, from the toes upward, acknowledging sensations, tension, or discomfort, and consciously inviting each area to relax. This method promotes a deep awareness of bodily sensations, facilitating a state of mental and physical peace essential for sound sleep (Sleep Meditation Using Guided Imagery - HelpGuide.org, 2021). Begin by removing distractions from your environment and lie down comfortably. With closed eyes, direct your focus to your toes, then gradually move up to your feet, legs, and so forth, noticing and relaxing each region. This not only alleviates physical tension but also redirects mental focus away from stress-inducing thoughts, further preparing the mind for rest (Nunez, 2020).

We understand it might take time to adjust to these practices. The key is consistency. Establish a meditation routine, even if it begins with just a few minutes each night, and gradually increase to ensure sustained benefits. The longer you dedicate to these methods, the more effectively you'll train your mind to associate meditation with sleep, creating a soothing prelude to rest (Nunez, 2020).

Incorporating meditation techniques into your nightly routine does more than prepare the body for sleep; it rewires the brain to better manage stress and emotions, contributing to overall psychological well-being. Over time, these practices enhance your ability to disconnect from the day's chaos, sparking a clearer mind and a more open heart to receive the gifts of rest (Nunez, 2020).

Take comfort in knowing there's no right or wrong way to meditate. **Experiment** with different techniques to find what resonates best with you and your lifestyle. By making meditation a regular part of your evening, you're extending an invitation for tranquility and respite, allowing your body to follow its natural path toward restorative sleep (Sleep Meditation Using Guided Imagery - HelpGuide.org, 2021).

The upcoming section explores the use of a bedside notebook as a tool to track thoughts related to sleep, which can add another layer of reflection to your bedtime meditation routine. This approach not only aids in clearing the mind but also provides insights into patterns that might be affecting your sleep, thereby enhancing the effectiveness of meditation techniques in your journey toward better rest.

Using Tools for Mindfulness and Reflection at Bedtime

I know I have said this before, but having a notebook by your bedside can be essential for those struggling with sleep, as it aids in becoming aware of emotions, supports personalized nightly strategies, and reinforces accountability in meditation practices. Documenting your emotions right before bed helps to identify triggers that may cause restlessness and allows you to clear your mind. Jotting down feelings like stress or anxiety offers a release, helping to calm the mind and declutter the mental space, which is essential for a peaceful night.

Take, for instance, when you're lying in bed and your mind is racing with thoughts of unfinished tasks. Writing them down transforms intangible worries into manageable lists, offering practical solutions. Your notebook becomes a tool for holding yourself accountable to a wind-down routine, enabling a smoother transition to sleep.

Maintaining an emotional diary helps in crafting personalized strategies for rest. Noticing a pattern where work-related stress often impedes sleep allows you to focus meditative practices towards these specific stressors. This reflection is crucial as it empowers you to adapt your approach until you find what works best for you.

Reflecting on nightly experiences in the journal can reveal patterns that need adjustment. You might notice that meditation some nights leads to better sleep than others. By recording the details of the day or the specifics of the meditation practice used, you can identify what consistently supports restful slumber.

A bedtime ritual where you reflect on meditation insights deepens understanding and commitment, pushing you closer to mastering sleep-oriented mindfulness. For example, after practicing a calming breathing meditation, noting sensations or thoughts that emerged helps in recognizing its effectiveness. These notes guide future meditative practices, aiding in refining styles that best promote tranquility.

This practice isn't just about examining what didn't work but also celebrating what did. If a technique successfully alleviated tension, then it's worth repeating. This reflective practice roots meditation in daily life, making it a habitual part of your evening rather than an occasional addition.

Incorporating gratitude lists into your notebook can help shift focus from anxiety to appreciation. By writing a few lines about what you're grateful for, you redirect your attention away from worries and towards positive reflections. For instance, listing three things from your day that brought you joy or peace fosters a sense of contentment.

Gratitude lists (as discussed in Chapter 3) encourage a mindset focused on abundance rather than lack, an ideal platform from which to enter sleep. Acknowledging not just significant moments, but small ones like enjoying a favorite meal or receiving a kind text message, fills your mind with pleasant memories.

To incorporate a bedside notebook effectively, begin with these steps:

- Document Emotions: Before sleep, take five minutes to write about your current feelings. Focus on identifying any emotional triggers encountered throughout the day.

- Track Sleep Experiences: Each morning, spend a moment capturing how well you slept, any dreams, disturbances, and the emotions felt upon waking.

- Reflect Meditation Insights: After each meditation, record any significant thoughts, sensations, or outcomes experienced during the session.

- List Gratitudes: Scribble three as a nightly habit, aiming to highlight positive aspects encountered during your day.

Consider the scenario where a busy parent finds themselves overwhelmed at bedtime. In practice, during times of stress, they might write: "My tension seems to ease with visualization meditations, imagining a peaceful forest." They may note, "Wanted to remember today's laughter during playtime — feeling thankful for these moments," thus reinforcing the positivity sought before sleep.

Recognizing progress through these exercises provides a framework for continued growth. As you're guided by your own words about what therapies worked or what needs change, a level of accountability is introduced that pushes for ongoing development. Recording events and evaluating patterns builds a useful repository of practices critical for overcoming sleep disruptions.

This consistent approach allows for an evaluative look at improving the quality of meditation practices, preparing readers for the nuances of tracking sleep adjustments and exploring different meditation styles in later chapters. Gratitude lists make transitions smooth, welcoming a peaceful bedside habit that primes minds for rest.

Building on mindfulness and relaxation techniques, creating a habit of journaling ensures that each day ends thoughtfully and begins with clarity. Rather than letting frustrations carry you away, the notebook becomes a safe space where experiences are organized, routines evaluated, and progress celebrated. This practice becomes especially valuable in settings where stress is abundant, but the release is scarce.

For a meaningful conclusion, balancing emotional awareness, documentation of nightly experiences, and gratitude listing opens a doorway into calmer, resilient nights, laying groundwork for exploring comprehensive ways to track and refine sleep patterns further. Eventually, maintaining this simple yet effective journaling routine prepares you not just for a better night's sleep, but a balanced, mindful way of living.

Personalized Sleep Tracking and Adjustment Strategies

Recognizing sleep patterns can be pivotal for making substantial changes to improve sleep quality. Monitoring these patterns allows individuals to identify the core issues affecting their rest, providing an opportunity to address specific concerns. For instance, you might notice that late night screen time corresponds with disrupted sleep, or that consuming caffeine after a certain hour impacts your ability to fall asleep. As discussed in Chapter 3, tracking helps you connect these dots over time, giving insight into your sleep habits that might otherwise go unnoticed.

When it comes to mapping out these patterns, keeping a detailed record of your daily activities and how they sync with your rest can make all the difference. Jot down what you eat, your exercise habits, and any stress-inducing activities. You may find, for example, that intense workouts right before bed keep you wired, while morning exercise enhances your sleep patterns. This meticulous approach reveals significant trends, allowing you to pinpoint what adjustments are needed both in your sleep environment and in your daily routine.

Documenting changes within your sleep environment stands as a crucial factor influencing your rest. Adjusting lighting could serve as an initial step. Perhaps dimming the lights a couple of hours before hitting the sack or investing in blackout curtains can reduce your exposure to artificial illumination, which often disrupts sleep cycles. Adding calming scents like lavender through essential oils to your bedroom might ease your transition into sleep by promoting relaxation. These modifications dovetail with sleep hygiene principles aimed at optimizing your restful experience.

Integrating these observations with journaling in a bedside notebook provides a comprehensive understanding of the factors affecting your sleep. Within the notebook, pen down thoughts and reflections from the day. Observing how mental stress or anxiety might infiltrate your rest or, conversely, how relaxation routines impact your sleep quality becomes easier when documented. It acts as a personal feedback loop, letting you fine-tune your approach to achieving restful sleep.

Maintaining consistency in sleep routines provides a bedrock for creating healthy sleep habits. It's vital to go to bed and wake up at the same time every day, even on weekends, to regulate your body's internal clock. If your routine deviates, whether due to social obligations or work, recognizing the effects of this variability empowers you to manage your expectations. For example, a temporary late night might require a calm next day, with an added wind-down period before bed to restore balance.

Connect lifestyle changes mindfully with noticeable sleep patterns. Tea substitutes for caffeine, for instance, might lead to an unexpected plunge in nightly wake-ups, demonstrating the interconnectedness between daily choices and sleep quality. A short evening walk could replace screen time, serving as a relaxing bridge to transition from the busyness of daily life to rest. This holistic adjustment looks at all contributors to sleep improvement, from stress management to diet and physical activity, promoting an overall healthier lifestyle.

Deciding which meditation practices suit your individual needs calls for a structured trial-and-error approach. Engage with several meditation styles, whether it be mindfulness meditation, guided meditation, or a body scan. For those new to meditation, start small with mini sessions to ease into a relaxation state. Set targeted goals to assess the effectiveness of these styles, perhaps focusing on falling asleep faster or waking up less during the night. Documenting outcomes after each session helps in discerning what impacts your sleep patterns favorably.

Sharing your meditative journey within a community offers broader insights, support, and accountability. Engaging with others who face similar challenges in wellness forums or support groups can provide motivational reinforcement and alternative strategies. Furthermore, hearing about the diverse experiences of others enriches your efforts to transform your sleep quality, fostering a collective sense of improvement.

Maintain simplicity and clarity, refraining from overcomplicating the process, and focusing instead on delivering actionable steps. Whether it's through aligning bedtime routines with natural circadian rhythms, experimenting with specific meditation techniques, or cultivating a supportive environment, each step forward solidifies your path toward better sleep. Accumulating these insights and practical efforts foster a commitment to improving your rest, enhancing your overall well-being.

Final Thoughts

In conclusion, integrating meditation techniques into your nightly routine offers a transformative path to improved sleep quality and overall well-being. These practices not only serve to quiet the mind and prepare the body for rest but also empower individuals to manage stress more effectively. By experimenting with mindfulness, guided visualization, breathwork, and body scans, you can discover the approach that resonates best with you. Consistent practice deepens your connection to relaxation, making it easier to disconnect from daily chaos and enter a peaceful state conducive to sleep. Now that we recognize the potential of these methods, our next step is to incorporate them regularly, adjusting as needed to suit personal preferences and lifestyle. As you continue this journey, remember that your commitment to meditation paves the way for deeper rest and renewed energy each day.

Chapter 11

Obtaining Medical Advice

I have consulted with numerous doctors. concerning insomnia. From my experience, it is essential to find a physician who genuinely addresses **your** specific sleep issues. For instance, visiting a sleep apnea specialist may lead to a narrow focus on breathing issues as the sole problem, overlooking other factors that could contribute to your insomnia. Similarly, consulting a mental health professional might result in the neglect of physical conditions affecting your sleep quality. Finding the right specialist, or even a generalist, is critical when trying to find a solution.

Identifying Trustworthy Healthcare

Earlier chapters took a deep dive into the dietary components crucial for good sleep hygiene, underscoring the significance of foods that are conducive to sleep and the timing of your meals. Now, we pivot to another pillar of healthy sleep practices: finding the right healthcare providers. Just as your food choices directly influence your sleep, who you choose to discuss your sleep issues with can also have a profound impact. Knowing whom to trust when it comes to sleep-related health care is essential for improving not just your sleep, but your overall quality of life.

The first step in this journey is identifying healthcare professionals who have specialized expertise in sleep issues. Much like choosing the right foods, selecting the right practitioner requires careful consideration. You're not just looking for any doctor; you're seeking someone who truly understands the nuances of sleep disorders. So how do you find them? Start by gathering a list of potential practitioners. Use online resources, talk to other health care providers, or seek recommendations from friends who have dealt with similar issues.

Arming yourself with the right questions is crucial in evaluating these providers. Are they certified in sleep medicine? What experience do they have with your type of sleep issue? Do they offer a range of treatments, from behavioral therapy to medication, and how flexible are they in adapting for personal needs? Asking these questions will help establish a foundation of trust and ensure you are in capable hands (Colten et al., 2006).

Researching a provider doesn't end with these questions. Online reviews can offer additional insights. However, it's important to weigh both positive and negative feedback carefully. An overwhelming number of negative reviews may be a sign to look elsewhere, but sometimes, you might find that the issues raised are not relevant to your situation. Positive reviews that highlight successful treatment of sleep problems similar to yours are promising but delve deeper. Were there consistent mentions of rapport and understanding between the caregiver and the patient? Did reviewers feel heard and respected during consultations? Details like these speak volumes and shouldn't be overlooked.

Understanding treatment options is also a key component of evaluating a practitioner. Traditional options are well-publicized, but alternative therapies are gaining attention as potential solutions. Acupuncture, cognitive behavioral therapy for insomnia, and even meditation practices have shown promise. Have an open discussion with your potential healthcare provider about these options. Do they support trying alternative treatments, and if so, which ones do they recommend? Understanding the available treatments helps you to assess their relevance to your needs and decide whether a provider's philosophy aligns with your own health goals.

Equally imperative is your role in advocating for your own health. Bringing documented sleep patterns or sleep diaries to your appointments can be an effective strategy in fostering strong communication with your healthcare provider (Gibson et al., 2022). Documenting your sleep routines and any disturbances you experience will give them tangible data to work with. This action might reveal patterns or trigger points you weren't previously aware of and allows you to engage in more productive discussions about causes and potential interventions.

Developing rapport with your chosen healthcare provider can greatly influence the success of your treatment. If you can speak candidly and feel truly listened to, you're more likely to continue adhering to treatment plans and provide valuable feedback. Mutual respect is key; it ensures that you both view your health as a collaborative endeavor rather than a hierarchy of instructions. To build this rapport, try to connect personally during your consultations. Share more than just surface-level concerns. Explain how your sleep issues are affecting your day-to-day life, and listen to how your provider plans to address these concerns (Colten et al., 2006).

To increase your confidence in making healthcare choices, don't hesitate to use additional methods to evaluate your options. For example, you might want to seek second opinions for a diagnosis or a proposed treatment plan. Different physicians may bring new perspectives, and exposing yourself to these can make your final decision more informed and intentional. Also, keep up with current research and new findings related to sleep disorders, as this can prompt you to revisit questions or raise new ones with your provider (Gibson et al., 2022).

The role of healthcare in managing sleep disorders is not to be underestimated. With chronic sleep issues affecting many, a specialized approach to diagnosis and treatment is paramount for both short-term relief and long-term health. The guidelines set out here provide a reliable means of navigating through the often complex process of selecting healthcare assistance for sleep troubles. By equipping yourself with the right questions, being diligent in your research, and advocating strongly for your needs, you can take charge of your sleep health.

Building a support network of sleep professionals who are committed to understanding and addressing your specific challenges will empower you to achieve your sleep goals. This, along with the strategic dietary changes explored earlier, forms a comprehensive approach to improving your sleep hygiene and, by extension, your overall well-being. Investing in these connections can yield profound benefits, bringing you closer to a more rested, healthier life.

Concluding Thoughts

This section shifts focus to a crucial element of healthy sleep practices: finding the right healthcare providers for sleep issues. It emphasized the importance of identifying specialists who understand **your specific** sleep disorders and provides guidance on how to evaluate potential practitioners. Questions about their qualifications, experience, and treatment options are essential for establishing trust. Additionally, researching online reviews and understanding different treatment methodologies, including alternative therapies, can help ensure alignment with personal health goals. Advocating for oneself and being prepared by bringing sleep documentation to appointments fosters effective communication and enables a collaborative relationship with healthcare providers. Overall, the selection of a knowledgeable practitioner and supportive network is vital for managing sleep disorders, alongside earlier discussed life-style strategies, to enhance overall well-being.

Chapter 12

The Summary Chapter: Combination Factors

Okay. So, now I am going on daily walks, I am on prescription medication for sleep, I take melatonin before bed, I turn off the television one-hour before sleep, and I spray jasmine oil on my pillow: is it working? Maybe? Do I need to change *one* thing? Do I need to change *multiple* things?

In exploring these questions, we're diving into the world of combination factors affecting sleep. This chapter sheds light on how seemingly unrelated (or related) elements come together to impact your nightly rest. By understanding the interplay of these factors, you'll gain insights into how various aspects of your environment, emotions, lifestyle choices, and health collectively shape the quality of your sleep. Through this journey, you're invited to consider personal influences and discover practical approaches that could potentially lead to better sleep experiences.

Combo Stimulation Contributors

Diving into the realm of sleep, we often find that its quality isn't just about getting the recommended seven to eight hours. Various elements come together to form the tapestry of what we understand as good or disrupted sleep. Central to these elements is the **physical environment.** Room temperature, for one, can make or break a night of quality rest. Cooler temperatures typically facilitate better sleep, as the body naturally seeks to lower its core temperature to initiate sleep. Meanwhile, excessive noise can easily disrupt sleep, especially for those who live in bustling urban settings where street noise, traffic, and even late-night shenanigans can pull anyone out of a deep slumber (Johnson et al., 2018). Light exposure, particularly blue light from screens, also interferes with our circadian rhythms, delaying the production of melatonin that prepares the body for sleep. Urban environments, with their plethora of artificial lights, often present this challenge, often more prominently for night owls and those with irregular sleep schedules (Billings et al., 2020).

The **emotional state** plays a considerable role in sleep quality. Stress and anxiety, often linked with insomnia, feed into a vicious cycle. Stressful thoughts can prevent the mind from unwinding, and the increased levels of cortisol hinder sleep onset. For example, those experiencing high stress at work might lie awake as they churn over the day's projects or tomorrow's tasks. Emotional health, therefore, becomes a determining factor. Anxiety disorders, where worry takes over completely, leave many struggling to fall or stay asleep, further impacting their quality of life and work performance (Johnson et al., 2018). Individuals with depression also report disturbances in sleep regulation. These emotional triggers set off a chain reaction, where poor sleep amplifies mood and mental health conditions, feeding back into disturbed sleep patterns.

Lifestyle choices add another layer of complexity. Physical activity, for instance, is a double-edged sword. Regular exercise can promote healthy sleep by stabilizing mood and decompressing stress, yet engaging in strenuous exercises close to bedtime may leave you too energized to sleep. Caffeine and alcohol consumption are other significant influencers. While caffeine stimulates the central nervous system, keeping you alert, alcohol, a depressant, might seem like it helps you unwind, but it typically reduces sleep quality and delays the REM stages (Billings et al., 2020). Meanwhile, meal timing can influence your body's clock. Eating heavy meals too close to bedtime might lead to discomfort and indigestion, reducing sleep readiness and quality. Each of these lifestyle habits can modulate the body's internal clock and establish new rhythms that either support or obstruct natural sleep cycles.

Health factors provide a further array of elements that intertwine intimately with the other contributors to sleep disruption. Chronic pain often interrupts sleep continuity. For individuals with conditions like arthritis or fibromyalgia, discomfort may increase in the evening, pushing the body into a state of arousal rather than relaxation (Johnson et al., 2018). One must analyse their bed to ensure they are having the require support to maintain comfort while sleeping. Mental health disorders, including depression and anxiety, not only impact mood but also tax the body physically, presenting a tangled web of interrelated symptoms that make it hard to rest. Sleep apnea, a disorder marked by interrupted breathing during sleep, exemplifies how specific health concerns can further complicate sleep patterns. The repeated start and stop of breathing can prevent the body from reaching a deep, restorative sleep, leaving individuals tired and weary despite seemingly sufficient hours of sleep.

Understanding these various elements requires an approach that keenly observes them in tandem rather than isolation. By examining their collective impact, individuals better appreciate the unique interplay between environmental, emotional, lifestyle, and health-related factors shaping their sleep. Employing self-assessment techniques forms a practical first step in this exploration. As discussed before, keeping a **sleep diary and/or a journal**, for instance, can provide insights into not only sleep patterns but also the presence and timing of specific triggers. Similarly, questionnaires can help identify underlying conditions or stressors affecting sleep quality (Billings et al., 2020).

Support systems, whether through a consistent social framework or professional guidance, often prove invaluable. Holistic approaches, embracing both medical treatments and lifestyle adaptations, offer pathways to address insomnia in multifaceted ways. This section integrates seamlessly with upcoming discussions centered around adopting systematic approaches. It encourages a methodical way to address sleep disturbances, urging readers to look toward future sections for guidance on how they can further parse out the interconnections identified here. With a focused effort on combining an awareness of supportive measures and personalized insights, individuals stand a better chance to improve the quality of their rest, delving deeper into the synergy of influencing factors.

The key takeaway lies in acknowledgment: recognizing that sleep is a complex, multi-dimensional process and approaching it with the understanding that no single factor operates in isolation. By channeling this comprehension into concrete actions, individuals can work towards bettering their sleep, ultimately enhancing their overall well-being and quality of life.

Finding Exact Combinations

To understand how various elements impact sleep, it's essential to explore personal factors contributing to restlessness. Most importantly, finding out which combinations of triggers affect your sleep empowers you to make informed changes. Start with practical methods that unravel these connections.

As discussed above, keeping a sleep diary (different from a journal) provides a straightforward way to track patterns between your lifestyle choices and nightly rest. Imagine each entry as a piece of a puzzle. It's not just about writing down when you go to bed and wake up but also noting interruptions, activities, meals, stress, and feelings throughout the day. Over time, entries can illustrate recurring themes. For example, you might notice that late-night snacks or stressful workdays affect sleep quality, leading to patterns worthy of attention (Rossman, 2019).

Utilizing self-questionnaires can also shed light on emotional and environmental factors impacting sleep. These assessments help identify mood influences and environmental stressors inhibiting restful slumber. Often, these tools spotlight triggers such as anxiety, room noise, or lighting. It might surprise someone to discover that their seemingly minor Sunday night blues, reflected as disrupted sleep patterns, could stem from Monday's looming responsibilities (Mayo Clinic, 2016).

Routine physical and mental health check-ins serve as a third method; minor fluctuations in physical health or emotional wellness can subtly affect sleep. It's like tuning a musical instrument. Small aches or mood dips often mirror changes in sleep, helping to pinpoint unusual patterns or potential disturbances.

Experimentation with sleep hygiene shows how minor changes may significantly enhance sleep quality. Begin with altering room temperature, swapping heavy blankets for lighter ones, or restricting screen time before bed. Each adaptation serves as an experiment aiming to understand its impact on sleep. Write down any noticeable improvements tied to these changes to help customize future habits. For instance, reducing evening screen time might finally achieve that elusive full night of sleep, as reflected in sleep diary entries (Rossman, 2019).

Building a robust support network of family, friends, and professionals can extend your understanding of sleep disruptors. These allies provide new insights or motivations to embark on unfamiliar routines. Consider a friend who could remind you not to scroll through the phone at night or a family member who encourages relaxation exercises before bed. Their perspectives contribute fresh ideas to the quest for better rest. Engagement with a therapist or sleep consultant can guide the identification of complex combinations, such as the interplay between emotional and physical factors (Mayo Clinic, 2016).

Holistic approaches demonstrate that integrating relaxation techniques with environmental changes ramps up results. For instance, combining progressive muscle relaxation exercises with removing distracting digital devices shows potential for calming both the mind and physical space. These multifaceted interventions amplify well-being by addressing sleep on emotional, psychological, and physical levels.

Here's a direct approach to keeping a sleep diary or using a sleep monitoring app:

- Place the diary near your bed.

- Document what time you go to bed and wake up each day, including overnight disruptions.

- Document medications, the amounts, and the time you take them.

- Include daily activities, meal times, significant events, emotional experiences, medications, drugs and alcohol.

- Weekly, look for connections between your daily choices and sleep quality results.

Explaining why emotional highs suddenly disrupt sleep or why meals affect slumber deepens one's understanding of personal triggers. Experimentation and methodical tracking allow you to piece together subtle influences and construct individualized strategies that tackle insomnia.

Lastly, I hope this journey equips you to recognize broader patterns and craft effective, well-informed strategies addressing overarching sleep challenges. Engaging actively in identification and experimentation blends insights gained from tracking, assessments, and support participation into an actionable framework for better sleep. Understanding these personal intricacies nurtures enhanced rest and lays the foundation for exploring less tangible influences on sleep such as cultural and psychological factors in future discussions.

Various Influencing Factors Mixing Together

Understanding how various influences intersect to affect sleep patterns can significantly benefit individuals seeking to manage sleep challenges. Previously, we explored self-assessment techniques, experimentation with changes, support systems, and holistic approaches, providing foundational insights into personal sleep dynamics. Drawing on that foundation, we must now identify specific influences: biological, psychological, social, and cultural, which may not be immediately apparent but are crucial for addressing sleep issues.

Genetic factors offer some of the most compelling insights into sleep patterns. Genetics determines how we sleep, from sleep-wake cycles to vulnerability to sleep disorders such as insomnia or restless legs syndrome. Studies elucidate associations between genetic markers and depression, revealing a complex interplay between genetic predispositions and sleep (Remes, 2021). For instance, genetic factors could predispose individuals to depression, influencing their ability to achieve restful sleep, thus exacerbating their mental health conditions. Recognizing these genetic influences helps guide necessary interventions.

The impact of hormonal changes, particularly during different life stages, presents another critical dimension. Women undergoing menopause experience drastic hormonal changes, contributing to sleep issues like night sweats and insomnia. Hormonal fluctuations disrupt the regularity of sleep patterns, demanding adjusted lifestyles to accommodate these changes. Such adjustments might include creating cooler sleep environments or incorporating relaxation techniques aimed at restoring hormonal balance. Understanding and addressing these changes is crucial for maintaining quality sleep.

Psychological stress remains a significant factor. Daily stressors like job pressures, familial obligations, and social commitments can heighten anxiety levels, making relaxation difficult at night. Such psychological stress often results in poor sleep quality, with sufferers unable to easily transition from a state of alertness to restfulness, resulting in fragmented sleep cycles. Recognizing stressors and employing stress-reduction techniques—such as mindfulness and relaxation exercises—are quintessential steps toward mitigating its adverse impact on sleep.

Social determinants contribute another layer. People encounter varying conditions based on their socioeconomic status, social support networks, and living environments, all of which significantly impact their sleep health (Remes, 2021). For those with poor resources, unstable living conditions or unsafe neighborhoods might lead to heightened vigilance and poor sleep quality. In contrast, strong social networks often provide emotional support, contributing positively to healthier sleep patterns. This contrast highlights the importance of social cohesion as a tool to mend sleep issues perturbing community members.

Cultural practices influence sleep in nuanced ways. A person's beliefs and attitudes about sleep, shaped by their culture, can heavily dictate their sleep behaviors (Grandner, 2017). For instance, some cultures endorse napping during the day, while others view all-day alertness as an ideal. These beliefs can affect sleep duration and quality, with significant implications for long-term health. The global integration of diverse cultures—enhanced by digital connectivity—adds layers to sleep-related cultural practices, allowing shifts that might embrace more productive sleep routines.

To provide concrete examples, consider how these factors might collectively impact a person's sleep. Take someone genetically predisposed to anxiety—a condition aggravated by stressful life events such as job insecurity. If that person lives in a high-strain socio-economic context, where work schedules are erratic and social support is scant, they face a compounded scenario. Factor in cultural norms that prioritize rising early and working long hours, and you have an individual caught in a multifaceted web affecting their sleep. Only by disentangling each contributing factor can effective interventions be strategized.

Avoiding redundancy in understanding this multi-layered approach is vital. We explored biological factors through genetics and hormonal changes, defined psychological influences through stress and anxiety, and outlined social elements by examining personal networks and economic conditions. Cultural influences are crucially distinct, laying a foundation for comprehending sleep disruptions holistically. This framework illuminates paths to examine sleep-related difficulties from every angle, ensuring readers understand that no single aspect exists in isolation; rather, they intertwine to impact the totality of sleep health.

This discussion preludes the next section, which will delve into personalized sleep hygiene strategies, advocating integrative techniques that reflect individuals' unique circumstances. Understanding one's multifactorial sleep inhibitors is the first step toward devising comprehensive, tailored solutions and promoting adaptability in sleep routines. The next exploration will leverage these insights, facilitating approaches that incorporate feedback loops and foster personal adaptability, setting the stage for improved sleep solutions designed around individual needs and characteristics. By equipping readers with these personalized strategies, we aspire to offer an empowered approach to managing their sleep, encouraging a proactive stance in fostering sleep health in their lives.

Customizing Sleep Solutions

Adults grappling with sleep issues often find that the solution lies not in targeting a single factor but in addressing multiple overlapping influences. Recognizing that our sleep quality reflects a combination of biological, psychological, and social factors requires a mindset shift towards embracing holistic approaches that integrate these diverse elements. This perspective encourages us to look beyond the singular focus on sleep quantity and instead consider how to improve sleep quality through understanding personalized, integrative techniques.

The interplay between psychological and social influences becomes evident when considering stress and its effect on sleep. Stress often exacerbates sleep problems and disrupts relaxation. By embracing integrative techniques and adapting routines, individuals can mitigate these effects. For example, (aside from techniques discussed earlier) progressive muscle relaxation combined with controlled breathing can significantly ease stress-induced insomnia. (This Body Scan technique was discussed in Chapter 10.) To practice this method:

1. Progress through each muscle group in your body, tensing and

then relaxing each group one by one, starting from your toes and moving up to the head.

2. Focus on your breathing; inhale deeply as you tense the muscles and exhale fully as you release.

This combination can lead to a more immediate and lasting relaxation by simultaneously addressing physical tension and promoting mental calm.

Environmental adjustments tailored to individual preferences offer another pathway to better sleep. For some, room temperature plays a crucial role in achieving comfort. Lowering the bedroom temperature or using breathable bedding materials can significantly influence sleep quality. Adjust the thermostat to a comfortable cool setting and consider using a fan or air purifier to ensure good air circulation, which can improve the overall sleep experience.

Beyond environmental factors, bedtime routines that cater to personal preferences contribute immensely to relaxation. For instance, an adult struggling to unwind might find solace in a hot bath infused with calming essential oils like lavender or chamomile. The warmth elevates body temperature and relaxes muscles, which, as the body subsequently cools, mimics the natural drop in body temperature that occurs during sleep onset. This transition can enhance the readiness for sleep.

However, merely aiming for relaxation is inadequate without understanding optimal sleep durations. While some individuals thrive on seven hours of sleep, others need close to nine to feel fully rested. The key lies in acknowledging these variations and ensuring that sleep duration aligns with personal bodily needs to avoid the detrimental effects of sleep deprivation or excessive sleep.

Emphasizing individualized methods, dietary choices can interact with sleep schedules for further benefits. Consuming foods rich in magnesium, like almonds or spinach, in the evening can support muscle relaxation and improve sleep quality. When combined with adjusting sleep schedules to align with natural circadian rhythms—such as going to bed and waking at the same time daily—these dietary modifications can lead to significant improvements.

Effective self-help exercises integrate these concepts through practical applications:

1. Create a pre-sleep ritual that combines physical and mental relaxation. For example, write down any persistent thoughts in a journal to clear the mind of clutter before sleep. Use a relaxing light in the bedroom, or use some ambient noise.

2. Limit electronic device use prior to bedtime. Instead, substitute exposure to screens with reading a physical book or listening to soft music to signal the body that it's time to wind down.

The benefit of <u>lifestyle modifications,</u> coupled with environmental changes, reinforces good sleep habits. Regular evaluation and documentation of these strategies ensure adaptability to any situational changes. Keeping a sleep journal, documenting bedtime routines, dietary intake, and any fluctuations in environmental conditions can enhance the commitment to sleep strategies.

Encouraging resilience and adaptability in sleep routines involves introducing experimentation. The concept of documenting changes facilitates identifying patterns and understanding how distinctive factors influence personal sleep patterns. One might discover that minimizing caffeine intake a few hours before bed significantly impacts sleep onset time, or that meditative practices included in pre-sleep rituals help in achieving deeper, more restful sleep.

Seeking feedback through journaling or consulting with a sleep expert can offer clarity and reinforce effective paths. Journals provide insight into successful strategies that can be repeated, leading to lasting sleep improvements. When professional guidance is sought, it can further tailor these strategies to fit personal goals, conditions, and physical characteristics.

Culture also plays a vital role. Our cultural backgrounds often influence sleep practices, perceptions, and attitudes, and understanding these elements can offer unique interventions. For example, practices like afternoon naps or "siestas," customary in some cultures, may offer benefits that could be adapted into different lifestyles to enhance total restorative sleep.

Blending relaxation methods like progressive muscle relaxation with other lifestyle elements may uncover combined benefits for those enduring sleep issues. By engaging in activities that align with personal cultural values while incorporating modern relaxation techniques, one can achieve a more cohesive sleep enhancement plan. Adding these techniques to some natural remedies, like Valerian Root, or Ashwaganda may also assist with relaxing. Then, as an alternative (last) resort, obtaining a prescription medication may be required, which could be a positive turning-point solving your sleep puzzle.

As the journey to improved sleep continues, establishing an attitude of openness towards examining various influences and practices becomes essential. This process not only provides tailored solutions but also fosters a more comprehensive understanding of how to achieve better sleep, emphasizing that the path to restful nights often requires exploring diverse avenues to unearth the most effective results.

Summary and Reflections

In understanding the intricate interplay of factors that affect sleep, from environmental to emotional, lifestyle, and health-related influences, we uncover a multifaceted picture of what it means to achieve restorative rest. Now armed with this knowledge, I hope you can begin crafting personalized sleep strategies that address their unique triggers. This journey involves experimenting with changes in daily habits, monitoring sleep patterns, and seeking supportive measures tailored to individual needs. By adopting a proactive approach that integrates these insights, you can begin to face sleep challenges that can transition toward improved sleep quality and overall well-being. As we move forward, this comprehensive understanding enables us to develop adaptable solutions that better align with each individual's life and needs, paving the way for healthier sleep and a more balanced life.

Conclusion

A s we draw this exploration of sleep to a close, it's essential to grasp the depth and breadth of what constitutes restful slumber. Sleep is not merely a function of how long we rest our heads on the pillow; it is an intricate dance of numerous factors working in harmony. Biological rhythms, psychological states, and environmental conditions all intertwine to shape our nightly repose. This complexity might seem daunting at first glance, but understanding it empowers us to approach sleep as a multifaceted phenomenon deserving of thoughtful consideration and intentional action.

Consider for a moment that the journey to improved sleep is not about setting a rigid bedtime or monitoring sleep stages obsessively. Instead, it's about recognizing how interconnected aspects of our daily lives influence our sleep quality. Stress levels, dietary choices, and even ambient noise contribute significantly to how well we rest each night. It's crucial to acknowledge that by tuning into these elements, we can unlock strategies tailored to our unique challenges.

Imagine implementing small lifestyle adjustments that collectively lead to transformative changes in your sleep health. Something as simple as integrating a brief journaling session into your day can help offload worries and clear mental clutter before bed. Likewise, introducing physical activity into a routine not only boosts overall health but also encourages more profound, uninterrupted sleep cycles. Mindful eating, too, plays its part—opting for magnesium-rich snacks instead of sugar-laden alternatives could be the key to stabilizing energy levels and promoting better rest.

Equally vital is tending to our emotional well-being. Many of us are familiar with the restless nights where racing thoughts keep us from drifting into the peaceful depths of slumber. Emotional health is intricately linked to sleep patterns, and allowing yourself space to address this facet can make a world of difference. Simple techniques like meditation or mindfulness exercises are powerful tools for calming the whirlpool of thoughts, making way for tranquil and restorative sleep. These practices encourage a mindset that embraces calmness, helping us leave the worries of the day behind when we most need to unwind.

In parallel, let's delve into the profound impact our surroundings have on our sleep. The environment we choose to rest in can either nurture or hinder sleep quality. Imagine transforming your bedroom into a haven—a sanctuary designed to entice and cradle you into deep slumber. Controlling variables such as light, sound, and temperature can drastically alter how restful your nights become. A cool, dark room free of distractions fosters an atmosphere conducive to sleep. Decluttering, using blackout curtains, and perhaps introducing soothing scents can all enhance this restful cocoon.

Ultimately, improving sleep isn't about dramatic overhauls or unachievable routines. It's about harnessing insights into the myriad influences on sleep and crafting a personal blueprint that honors **your** unique needs. By embracing a holistic perspective—one that acknowledges the interplay of biological, psychological, and environmental factors—we can cultivate an empowering relationship with sleep. It becomes less of a mystery and more of a harmonious element woven seamlessly into the fabric of our daily lives.

Let this conclusion be an invitation for you to embark on your journey towards better sleep. Explore the nuances, try out different approaches, and fine-tune your habits until they resonate with your lifestyle. Remember, it's not about perfection but rather progress and self-compassion. Each step, no matter how small, brings you closer to nights filled with rejuvenation and days brimming with vitality.

As you take control of your sleep narrative, celebrate the victories along the way. Understand that setbacks may occur, yet persistence and a willingness to adapt pave the road to success. With the knowledge gained through examining the complexities surrounding sleep, you are now equipped to make informed decisions that cater to your own sleep sanctuary.

As we conclude this exploration into the nuances of sleep, remember that achieving restful nights stems from understanding its intrinsic complexity. Embrace hope and curiosity as you move forward. Your mindful engagement with the art of sleeping well holds the power to transform your nights and elevate your everyday life. Empower yourself with knowledge about how different factors intricately weave together, influencing your sleep quality. Implement practical, sustained changes to lifestyle habits, engender emotional peace, and nurture your physical surroundings. Remember, you are not alone. With each step forward, you inch closer to embracing sleep's full potential—a gift yielding vitality, clarity, and perhaps most importantly, a greater sense of well-being.

References

Alnawwar, M. A. (2023, August 16). *The effect of physical activity on sleep quality and sleep disorder: A systematic review.* Cureus. https://doi.org/10.7759/cureus.43595

Alshoaibi, Y., Bafil, W., & Rahim, M. (2023, July 1). *The effect of screen use on sleep quality among adolescents in Riyadh, Saudi Arabia.* Journal of Family Medicine and Primary Care. https://doi.org/10.4103/jfmpc.jfmpc_159_23

Andersen, M. L., Gabriel Natan Pires, & Tufik, S. (2024, February 20). *The Impact of Sleep: From Ancient Rituals to Modern Challenges.* Sleep Science; Brazilian Association of Sleep and Latin American Federation of Sleep Societies. https://doi.org/10.1055/s-0043-1777785

Anderson, K. N. (2018, January). *Insomnia and cognitive behavioural therapy—how to assess your patient and why it should be a standard part of care.* Journal of Thoracic Disease. https://doi.org/10.21037/jtd.2018.01.35

Balban, M. Y., Neri, E., Kogon, M. M., Weed, L., Nouriani, B., Jo, B., Holl, G., Zeitzer, J. M., Spiegel, D., & Huberman, A. D. (2023, January 10). *Brief structured respiration practices enhance mood and reduce phys-*

iological arousal. Cell Reports Medicine. https://doi.org/10.1016/j.xc rm.2022.100895

Billings, M. E., Hale, L., & Johnson, D. A. (2020, May). *Physical and Social Environment Relationship With Sleep Health and Disorders.* Chest. https://doi.org/10.1016/j.chest.2019.12.002

Buonanno, G., Canale, L., Solomon, M. T., Smith, M. G., & Stabile, L. (2024, August 1). *Effect of bedroom environment on sleep and physiological parameters for individuals with good sleep quality: a pilot study.* Building and Environment; Elsevier BV. https://doi.org/10.1016/j.bu ildenv.2024.111994

Casagrande, M., Forte, G., Favieri, F., & Corbo, I. (2022, July 11). *Sleep Quality and Aging: A Systematic Review on Healthy Older People, Mild Cognitive Impairment and Alzheimer's Disease.* International Journal of Environmental Research and Public Health. https://doi.org/10.3390/ ijerph19148457

Cheung, B. Y., Takemura, K., Ou, C., Gale, A., & Heine, S. J. (2021, April 26). *Considering cross-cultural differences in sleep duration between Japanese and Canadian university students* (A. Senju, Ed.). PLOS ONE. https://doi.org/10.1371/journal.pone.0250671

CNN, K. H. (2022, January 9). *How our ancestors used to sleep can help the sleep-deprived today.* CNN. https://www.cnn.com/2022/01/09/h ealth/sleep-history-wellness-scn/index.html

Colten, H. R., Altevogt, B. M., & Research, I. of M. (US) C. on S. M. and. (2006). *Improving Awareness, Diagnosis, and Treatment of Sleep Disorders.* Www.ncbi.nlm.nih.gov; National Academies Press (US). h ttps://www.ncbi.nlm.nih.gov/books/NBK19963/

Crocq, M.-A. (2007, December). *Historical and cultural aspects of man's relationship with addictive drugs*. Https://Www.dialogues-Cns.org/Contents-9-4/. https://doi.org/10.31887/dcns.2007.9.4/macrocq

Cronkleton, E. (2024, May 17). *10 breathing exercises to try when you're feeling stressed*. Healthline. https://www.healthline.com/health/breathing-exercise

Courtney, R. (2020, January 15). *Breathing retraining in sleep apnoea: a review of approaches and potential mechanisms*. Sleep and Breathing. https://doi.org/10.1007/s11325-020-02013-4

Davis, L. K., Bumgarner, J. R., Nelson, R. J., & Fonken, L. K. (2023, October 1). *Health Effects of Disrupted Circadian Rhythms by Artificial Light at Night*. Policy Insights from the Behavioral and Brain Sciences; SAGE Publishing. https://doi.org/10.1177/23727322231193967

Dingley, C., Daugherty, K., Derieg, M. K., & Persing, R. (2020). *Improving Patient Safety Through Provider Communication Strategy Enhancements*. Nih.gov; Agency for Healthcare Research and Quality (US). https://www.ncbi.nlm.nih.gov/books/NBK43663/

Doherty, Ronan et al., (2023). *The Impact of Kiwifruit Consumption on the Sleep and Recovery of Elite Athletes*. https://pmc.ncbi.nlm.nih.gov/articles/PMC10220871/

Drake, C., Roehrs, T., Shambroom, J., & Roth, T. (2013, November 15). *Caffeine Effects on Sleep Taken 0, 3, or 6 Hours before Going to Bed*. Journal of Clinical Sleep Medicine. https://doi.org/10.5664/jcsm.3170

Duan, J., Li, Q., Yin, Z., Zhen, S., Cao, W., Yan, S., Zhang, Y., Wu, Q., Zhang, W., & Liang, F. (2024, November 20). *Outdoor Artificial Light at Night and Insomnia-Related Social Media Posts.* JAMA Network Open; American Medical Association. https://doi.org/10.1001/jaman etworkopen.2024.46156

Emmitt, S. (2023, September 1). *Exploring the nexus between bedroom design and sleep quality in a warming climate.* Urban Climate. https:/ /doi.org/10.1016/j.uclim.2023.101635

Fitzgerald, T., & Vietri, J. (2015). *Residual Effects of Sleep Medications Are Commonly Reported and Associated with Impaired Patient-Reported Outcomes among Insomnia Patients in the United States.* Sleep Disorders. https://doi.org/10.1155/2015/607148

Fortis.seo@fortishealthcare.com. (2024). *Fortis Healthcare Ltd.* Fortis Healthcare. https://www.fortishealthcare.com/blogs/relationship-between-sl eep-patterns-and-psychological-well-being-workplace-dr-shambhavi

Fuller, C., Lehman, E., Hicks, S., & Novick, M. B. (2017, October 27). *Bedtime Use of Technology and Associated Sleep Problems in Children.* Global Pediatric Health. https://doi.org/10.1177/2333794x17736972

Gibson, C., Smith, D., & Morrison, A. K. (2022, April). *Improving health literacy knowledge, behaviors, and confidence with interactive training.* HLRP: Health Literacy Research and Practice. https://doi.o rg/10.3928/24748307-20220420-01

Grandner, M. A. (2017, March). *Sleep, Health, and Society.* Sleep Medicine Clinics. https://doi.org/10.1016/j.jsmc.2016.10.012

Hardavella, G., Aamli-Gaagnat, A., Frille, A., Saad, N., Niculescu, A., & Powell, P. (2017). *Top Tips to Deal with Challenging situations: Doc-*

tor–patient Interactions. Breathe. https://doi.org/10.1183/20734735. 006616

Hah, R. (2024) *The Best — and Worst — Sleep Positions for Back Pain*. https://www.keckmedicine.org/blog/the-best-and-worst-sleep-positio ns-for-back-pain/

Hale, L. (2018, April 27). *Youth Screen Media Habits and Sleep*. Child and Adolescent Psychiatric Clinics of North America. https://doi.org /10.1016/j.chc.2017.11.014

Health, G. (2024, December 7). *Understanding Anxiety-In-duced Insomnia and Tips for Better Sleep*. Good Health Psych | Psychiatric Services for Adults, and Adolescents in NYC. https://goodhealthpsych.com/blog/anxiety-induced-insomnia -understanding-the-connection-and-how-to-heal/

Homemakers Furniture. (2024). *Homemakers.com*. https://www.homemakers.com/blog/ideas-and-advice/bedroom-color -psychology-explore-how-colors-affect-sleep-and-mood.html?srsltid=A fmBOoqKOKT-wHji9HA_AGDYQaE1t2QZIh5Kt9yJ3gCO6TeLos XQ37Ig

Höhn, C., Hahn, M. A., Gruber, G., Pletzer, B., Cajochen, C., & Hoedl-moser, K. (2024, May 17). *Effects of evening smartphone use on sleep and declarative memory consolidation in male adolescents and young adults*. Brain Communications; Oxford University Press. https://doi.org/10. 1093/braincomms/fcae173

Höhn, C., Schmid, S. R., Plamberger, C. P., Bothe, K., Angerer, M., Gruber, G., Pletzer, B., & Hoedlmoser, K. (2021, January 22). *Prelimi-nary Results: The Impact of Smartphone Use and Short-Wavelength Light during the Evening on Circadian Rhythm, Sleep and Alertness.* Clocks & Sleep. https://doi.org/10.3390/clockssleep3010005

Johnson, D. A., Billings, M. E., & Hale, L. (2018, May 5). *Environmental Determinants of Insufficient Sleep and Sleep Disorders: Implications for Population Health.* Current Epidemiology Reports. https://doi.org/1 0.1007/s40471-018-0139-y

Korkutata, A., Korkutata, M., & Lazarus, M. (2025, February 3). *The impact of exercise on sleep and sleep disorders.* Npj Biological Timing and Sleep; Nature Publishing Group. https://doi.org/10.1038/s44323-024 -00018-w

Lee, D., Jang, T., Kim, H., & Kang, M. (2021, January). *The relationship between working hours and lifestyle behaviors: Evidence from a population-based panel study in Korea.* Journal of Occupational Health. https://doi.org/10.1002/1348-9585.12280

Levendowski, D. J., Gamaldo, C., St. Louis, E. K., Ferini-Strambi, L., Hamilton, J. M., Salat, D., Westbrook, P. R., & Berka, C. (2019, January 22). *Head Position During Sleep: Potential Implications for Patients with Neurodegenerative Disease.* Journal of Alzheimer's Disease. https://do i.org/10.3233/jad-180697

Li, J., Vitiello, M. V., & Gooneratne, N. S. (2017, November 21). *Sleep in Normal Aging.* Sleep Medicine Clinics. https://doi.org/10.1016/j.j smc.2017.09.001

Liang, Z., Melcer, E., Kingkarn Khotchasing, Chen, S., Hwang, D., & Hoang, N. H. (2024, September 23). *Game On for Zzz's: The Role of Relevance in Shaping Perceptions of Sleep Hygiene Games Among Uni-*

versity Students (Preprint). JMIR Serious Games; JMIR Publications. https://doi.org/10.2196/64063

Lin, T., Ping, Y., Jing, C. M., Xu, Z. X., & Ping, Z. (2025, January 8). *The efficacy of internet-based cognitive behavior therapy for psychological health and quality of life among breast cancer patients: a systematic review and meta-analysis*. Frontiers in Psychology; Frontiers Media. https://doi.org/10.3389/fpsyg.2024.1488586

Mayo Clinic. (2016, September 28). *Insomnia treatment: Cognitive behavioral therapy instead of sleeping pills*. Mayo Clinic. https://www.mayoclinic.org/diseases-conditions/insomnia/in-depth/insomnia-treatment/art-20046677

Memon, J., & Manganaro, S. N. (2021). *Obstructive Sleep-disordered Breathing*. PubMed; StatPearls Publishing. https://www.ncbi.nlm.nih.gov/books/NBK441909/

Nunn, C. L., Samson, D. R., & Krystal, A. D. (2016, July 28). *Shining evolutionary light on human sleep and sleep disorders*. Evolution, Medicine, and Public Health. https://doi.org/10.1093/emph/eow018

Nunez, K. (2020, January 13). *Meditation for Sleep: How to Use Meditation for Insomnia, Better Sleep*. Healthline. https://www.healthline.com/health/meditation-for-sleep

Park, S.-Y., Oh, M.-K., Lee, B.-S., Kim, H.-G., Lee, W.-J., Lee, J.-H., Lim, J.-T., & Kim, J.-Y. (2015). *The Effects of Alcohol on Quality of Sleep*. Korean Journal of Family Medicine. https://doi.org/10.4082/kjfm.2015.36.6.294

Palagini, L., Miniati, M., Caruso, V., Alfi, G., Geoffroy, P. A., Domschke, K., Riemann, D., Gemignani, A., & Pini, S. (2024, January 1). *Insomnia, anxiety and related disorders: A systematic review on clinical and therapeutic perspective with potential mechanisms underlying their complex link*. Neuroscience Applied; Elsevier BV. https://doi.org/10.1016/j.nsa.2024.103936

Pavithra, S., Aich, A., Chanda, A., Zohra, I. F., Gawade, P., & Das, R. K. (2024, January 1). *PER2 gene and its association with sleep-related disorders: A review*. Physiology & Behavior. https://doi.org/10.1016/j.physbeh.2023.114411

Quante, M., Khandpur, N., Kontos, E. Z., Bakker, J. P., Owens, J. A., & Redline, S. (2019, August). *"Let's talk about sleep": a qualitative examination of levers for promoting healthy sleep among sleep-deprived vulnerable adolescents*. Sleep Medicine. https://doi.org/10.1016/j.sleep.2018.10.044

Remes, O. (2021, December 10). *Biological, psychological, and social determinants of depression: A review of recent literature*. Brain Sciences. https://doi.org/10.3390/brainsci11121633

Robinson, T., Condell, J., Ramsey, E., & Leavey, G. (2023, February 1). *Self-Management of Subclinical Common Mental Health Disorders (Anxiety, Depression and Sleep Disorders) Using Wearable Devices*. International Journal of Environmental Research and Public Health. https://doi.org/10.3390/ijerph20032636

Roehrs, T., & Roth, T. (2024). *Sleep, Sleepiness, and Alcohol Use*. Alcohol Research & Health. https://pmc.ncbi.nlm.nih.gov/articles/PMC6707127/

Rusch, H. L., Rosario, M., Levison, L. M., Olivera, A., Livingston, W. S., Wu, T., & Gill, J. M. (2018, December 21). *The effect of mindfulness meditation on sleep quality: a systematic review and meta-analysis of randomized controlled trials.* Annals of the New York Academy of Sciences. https://doi.org/10.1111/nyas.13996

Sabiniewicz, A., Zimmermann, P., Ozturk, G. A., Warr, J., & Hummel, T. (2022, October 13). *Effects of odors on sleep quality in 139 healthy participants.* Scientific Reports. https://doi.org/10.1038/s41598-022 -21371-5

Scullin, M. K., Krueger, M. L., Ballard, H. K., Pruett, N., & Bliwise, D. L. (2018, January 1). *The effects of bedtime writing on difficulty falling asleep: A polysomnographic study comparing to-do lists and completed activity lists.* Journal of Experimental Psychology: General. https://doi .org/10.1037/xge0000374

Sejbuk, M., Mirończuk-Chodakowska, I., & Witkowska, A. M. (2022, May 2). *Sleep Quality: A Narrative Review on Nutrition, Stimulants, and Physical Activity as Important Factors.* Nutrients. https://doi.org/10.3 390/nu14091912

Smit, A. N., Broesch, T., Siegel, J. M., & Mistlberger, R. E. (2019, November 21). *Sleep timing and duration in indigenous villages with and without electric lighting on Tanna Island, Vanuatu.* Scientific Reports. https://doi.org/10.1038/s41598-019-53635-y

Summer, J., & Guo, L. (2020, November 6). *Nutrition and Sleep: Diet's Effect on Sleep.* Sleep Foundation. https://www.sleepfoundation.org/n utrition

Summer, J. (2023, May 16). *What Color Helps You Sleep?* Sleep Foundation. https://www.sleepfoundation.org/bedroom-environment/what-color-helps-you-sleep

Suni, E. (2023, March 9). *Smell and Sleep: How Scents Can Affect Sleep.* Sleep Foundation. https://www.sleepfoundation.org/bedroom-environment/how-smell-affects-your-sleep

Suni, E., & Singh, A. (2022, April 18). *Technology in the Bedroom.* Sleep Foundation. https://www.sleepfoundation.org/bedroom-environment/technology-in-the-bedroom

Tamar Glatman Zaretsky, Jagodnik, K. M., Barsic, R., Josimar Hernandez Antonio, Bonanno, P. A., MacLeod, C., Pierce, C., Carney, H., Morrison, M. T., Saylor, C., Danias, G., Lepow, L., & Yehuda, R. (2024, April 1). *The Psychedelic Future of Post-Traumatic Stress Disorder Treatment.* Current Neuropharmacology; Bentham Science Publishers. https://doi.org/10.2174/1570159x22666231027111147

Timmermann, C., Roseman, L., Schartner, M., Milliere, R., Williams, L. T. J., Erritzoe, D., Muthukumaraswamy, S., Ashton, M., Bendrioua, A., Kaur, O., Turton, S., Nour, M. M., Day, C. M., Leech, R., Nutt, D. J., & Carhart-Harris, R. L. (2019, November 19). *Neural correlates of the DMT experience assessed with multivariate EEG.* Scientific Reports. https://doi.org/10.1038/s41598-019-51974-4

Vora, L. K., Gholap, A. D., Hatvate, N. T., Padmashri Naren, Khan, S., Chavda, V. P., Balar, P. C., Gandhi, J., & Dharmendra Kumar Khatri. (2024, August 1). *Essential Oils for Clinical Aromatherapy: A comprehensive review.* Journal of Ethnopharmacology; Elsevier BV. https://doi.org/10.1016/j.jep.2024.118180

Why. (2024, March 25). *The Path.* the Path. https://www.thepath.com/blog/2024/3/13/what-is-dmt-breath work-what-it-is-amp-why-you-should-try-it

Ye, J., Jia, X., Zhang, J., & Guo, K. (2022, September 26). *Effect of physical exercise on sleep quality of college students: Chain intermediary effect of mindfulness and ruminative thinking.* Frontiers in Psychology. https://doi.org/10.3389/fpsyg.2022.987537

Zee, P. C., Bertisch, S. M., Morin, C. M., Pelayo, R., Watson, N. F., Winkelman, J. W., & Krystal, A. D. (2023, January 1). *Long-Term Use of Insomnia Medications: An Appraisal of the Current Clinical and Scientific Evidence.* Journal of Clinical Medicine. https://doi.org/10.3390 /jcm12041629

www.ingramcontent.com/pod-product-compliance
Lightning Source LLC
Chambersburg PA
CBHW061603120626
46550CB00004B/1601